Boot Polish, Bears and Bush Sense

Adventures of a British Columbia Conservation Officer

Keith Rande

Boot Polish, Bears and Bush Sense
Copyright © 2020 by Keith Rande

tellwell

Tellwell Talent
www.tellwell.ca

ISBN
978-0-2288-3022-1 (Paperback)
978-0-2288-3023-8 (eBook)

For all those in enforcement who protect
us or the environment every day.

TABLE OF CONTENTS

PROLOGUE

The dogs had been gone five minutes now, and I was getting a little worried and frankly a bit frustrated at their quiet disappearance. As I turned back to mention this to the guys, John pointed past me, quietly saying he thought he had just heard something ahead of us. At that instant, from fifteen feet away, a brown blur exploded out of the underbrush and headed straight for me.

It was so low to the ground, I thought it was Major returning. Then, as fast as that thought entered my mind, I realized this was no dog. This was a grizzly coming in on a headlong charge. With my rifle at hip level, I pivoted it toward the bear and hollered, "Shoot!" while instinctively pulling hard on the trigger once, then twice ... But nothing happened. I was shocked. My trusty old rifle was failing me when I needed it most. The grizzly was closing in at lightning speed, and my rifle would not fire, no matter how hard I pulled the trigger. We were in serious trouble.

PREFACE

The experiences of a conservation officer (CO) in British Columbia, Canada, are as exciting and diverse as the province's fish and wildlife populations, geography and environments. From bears to bad guys, songbirds to salmon, they all offer their own unique challenges. Love of the natural environment and the desire to preserve it as best we can during our short time on this land is what attracts men and women to the CO role. An appreciation of the land and a desire to keep bad things from happening to our fish, wildlife and natural resources were the motivators for me. So, if you love nature and enjoy protecting the public, the environment and all its natural wonders (and money is not your only career motivator) then conservation law enforcement may be the right choice for you too.

I began my government career in the fish and wildlife field at the age of twenty. Growing up learning to love the outdoors, Dad and I spent countless hours hunting, fishing, cutting firewood and spending time outside. I always knew I wanted a career in the outdoors, telling Mom and Dad at a young age that I wanted to be a "naturalist" (not really knowing what that meant). I had always been fairly handy and crafty, so when I graduated from high school in Kamloops in 1977 a dental lab hired me to make gold and porcelain crowns and bridges. The dentists who owned the lab were friends with my high school agriculture teacher, Nick. They were looking for someone reliable to learn the trade, so he put in a good word for me. I enjoyed working with my hands fabricating the gold teeth, and I was quick to learn the trade, but every day I would sit looking out the window into the back alley, daydreaming about spending time in the woods.

Following my instincts, in 1979 I landed a summer job with the BC Fish and Wildlife Branch in Kamloops as a fisheries technician. I followed that up with a two-year environmental science program at Lethbridge Community College while continuing to work with the Fish and Wildlife Branch during the summer months. After graduating in 1981, I went back to work as a fish technician in Kamloops but soon took a shine to the work I saw the COs doing. I began applying for CO postings, and in 1983, I finally landed my first CO job and spent six months training in Kamloops. During my career, I was posted in Merritt, Squamish, Dawson Creek, Fort St. John and twice in Bella Coola.

Though I always thoroughly enjoyed catching resource abusers, it was dealing with the wildlife that usually provided the real entertainment for me. Accordingly, many of the stories in this book involve wildlife. Unfortunately, my duties as a CO often included euthanizing wildlife for a variety of reasons. My intent is certainly not to offend anyone when a reference is made to this type of activity; it was simply a non-glamorous but realistic part of our roles as COs.

The impetus for putting pen to paper and documenting a few of my memorable work experiences came mainly from family members. On countless occasions, after recounting an interesting day on the job, I would hear, "You need to write a book before you forget that!" As the years progressed, and I began to realize how special and interesting a CO's field experiences can be, I decided there might be something to what my family was saying. Perhaps this book will inspire other officers to write down their experiences too.

Deciding on a title for this collection of stories was not difficult. I was always proud of my uniform and tried to at least start my day with a pressed shirt, clean pants and shined boots. Over the years I had one or two other officers give me the gears about having clean, shined boots, and how that meant I probably was not spending enough time in the field. Nothing could have been further from the truth. Wanting and needing a clean, professional appearance as a peace officer was the reason for my uniform's state.

Secondly, handling and dealing with bears take up a large part of any British Columbia CO's career. Ask any CO, and the bear stories are endless. My experience was no different. I have chosen only a small handful of my more interesting bear stories to pass on.

Lastly, having a natural sixth sense, or bush savvy, when handling wildlife complaints or conducting field investigations into wildlife, fish or environmental offences is definitely an asset to a CO. Conservation Officers are often relied upon for their bush knowledge and expertise when other agencies have situations that take them into the field for one reason or another.

These tales are all true, however, a few names of members of the public have escaped me. In those cases (and there are not many), I have replaced their names in order to recount the story. If I have forgotten or mistaken some element of a story that involves another officer, I apologize.

The purpose of this book is not to detail the career of a British Columbia conversation officer, as the serious and detailed investigations, seizures, search warrants, patrols, and wildlife complaints would be countless. I simply want to pass on a few of the more memorable experiences from my CO time that folks might find interesting. A couple of the stories are serious, but many will likely touch your funny bone a bit. Some are a little sad, but most have an interesting aspect or unexpected twist. As in any COs career, the enjoyable and exhilarating experiences I have had have been countless over the years. I hope you enjoy reading them as much as I did experiencing and now recounting them.

ACKNOWLEDGEMENTS

I am thankful to my wife, Shannon, my son, Brycen, and my daughter, Nicole, for their years of patience with me. They encouraged me to write this book and took the time to help edit it. During my first ten years as a CO, I spent more time away from home working than at home with Shannon and the kids. I would put my hand up for every project that came my way. Also, I cannot count the number of times Shannon found frozen critters lying in the freezer that I had brought home from a complaint. She was always telling me to get them out of there. Shannon also kept me in ironed uniform shirts for the duration of my career.

I always figured moving around the province would provide Brycen and Nicole with a good variety of experiences and memories, which might then give them some insight when they ultimately chose an area of the province to reside in as adults. I think it did assist them, and they also enjoyed the variety of live animals I brought home over the years. However, moving from school to school also took a toll on their friendships.

I want to thank Mom and Dad for getting me into fishing and hunting when I was young. It kept me occupied and exposed me to the environment I came to enjoy. John Cartwright first hired me on with the Fish and Wildlife Branch in 1979. Thanks, John.

Additionally, I must thank Gerry Paull, Leo Van Tine and Ann Sutherland who rolled the dice and provided me with my first CO opportunity in 1983.

Thanks go out to all the conservation and fishery officers who I enjoyed working with over the years, including those involved or not involved with these tales. You know who you are. Also, I would like to thank the many RCMP officers I had the pleasure to work with in my various postings, and who backed me up on many occasions.

1

OF MOOSE
AND ALIENS

In the 1990s, wildlife was abundant in the Peace River area of British Columbia. The sheer number of wildlife species, combined with the vast number of crops on agricultural land, made the wildlife extremely visible, and at times vulnerable. This not only made Dawson Creek an extremely busy area for investigating hunting-related wildlife violations, but also for managing problem wildlife issues.

Although the highways in the Peace are straight and flat, much like those of the Prairie Provinces, countless deer, moose and elk were stuck, injured or killed by vehicles every year. It always seemed odd to me, with visibility being so good in the Peace, that so many ungulates were struck in broad daylight. With both mule and whitetail deer, you can always rely on a second deer bolting across the road once the first deer has already crossed. Many folks do not anticipate this, and once a single deer has cleared the road, folks put the pedal to the metal again, only to strike the second deer as it suddenly bolts onto the roadway.

Moose are especially dangerous, as their long legs put their heavy bodies higher from the ground, well above the hood level of most small cars. At a high rate of speed, a 900-pound moose does a great deal of damage when it rolls over the hood and comes through the windshield. So, while deer are almost always stopped by a car's grill or flung off to the side, over the years numerous people have lost their lives in moose collisions during the dark Peace Country winter nights. Being black, a moose entering or on the road is almost invisible at night, except for its long legs which are light grey on the lower half. Often, it is the legs that are seen first just before making contact with a moose. By then, it's usually too late to avoid the collision.

This, of course, meant that orphaned wildlife were commonplace in the Peace, and every spring many orphaned deer fawns and moose calves were reported and turned in by the public. We were on call 24/7 for our work. I recall one spring night at some ungodly hour a ringing phone jarring me and Shannon out of a dead sleep. Staggering over to the phone, which was plugged in on the far side of the bedroom, I managed to mumble a hello and found our twenty-four-hour live answering service on the other end. The friendly operator apologized for calling at such an awful hour and advised me that she had a woman on the line who wanted to report a fawn deer. Often, orphaned wildlife calls at night were associated with vehicle collisions, which involved the driver or the RCMP waiting at the roadside for a CO to attend and pick up or even dispatch an injured adult animal, or deal with an orphan. Patching me through to the caller I again said hello and asked the lady about the nature of her call.

The pleasant voice on the other end of the line said, "I'd like to report a fawn deer."

By now the last remnants of sleep were passing, and I was starting to comprehend what was being said. In anticipation of hearing about a vehicle collision and possibly having to attend a callout of some sort in the middle of the night, my response was, "Hi, okay … and …?"

The caller's pleasant voice answered, "I just wanted to report a fawn deer at the side of the road."

In anticipation, my response was once again, "Okay … and …?"

"No, nothing," she continued. "I was just driving down the Old Hart Highway and saw a fawn at the side of the road and wanted to report it."

"And is there an accident or an injured animal that requires the attendance of an officer?"

"No, I just wanted to report the fawn I saw at the side of the road when I was driving down the Old Hart Highway."

"And have you picked up the fawn and need an officer to take it off your hands or something?"

"No, I just wanted to report the fawn at the side of the road."

"You called in at three o'clock in the morning to report *seeing* a fawn deer at the side of the road … that's it?"

"Well … yes."

The call abruptly ended there, and I fell back into bed groaning and muttering words that I won't repeat at this time. I always took pride in being pleasant with the general public, rarely becoming agitated unless pressed hard by a bad guy or some other indignant person. However, in this case, I made a rare exception. I'm sure that pleasant, well-meaning lady on the other end of the phone still suffers to this day from a hearing disability in one ear from the high decibel level she experienced when my telephone receiver made contact with the phone set.

My point is our problem wildlife encounters came to us in many different ways, and many were the result of traffic collisions. For some reason, in 1996 the area I was working in experienced a high number of moose collisions resulting in orphaned calves. Dawson Creek was fortunate to have a wildlife rehabilitation centre that handled orphaned wildlife, and that year the count was at least seven calf moose. Calf moose were relatively easy to care for once they were over a few months old; the odd bundle of willow branches would keep them fed and happy. For some reason though, small calf moose were quite susceptible to stress and could die quickly and easily from it.

That year my ten-year-old nephew Derek was up visiting, and I took him along on an orphaned wildlife complaint to move a small calf moose to the rehab centre. I managed to blindfold the little duffer and tie its legs so it could not flail or struggle in the rear of the pickup. I put Derek in the pickup box with it for the short ride, and away we went. Of course, Derek was a happy camper sitting in the pickup box with the moose, gingerly stroking its head and body, reassuring the little guy that it was OK. Ten minutes later when we arrived, the calf was stone dead, sadly bursting Derek's newly obtained bubble. I reassured him he had done nothing wrong, and that the little moose had probably died from the stress of being handled. Nonetheless, he was affected by the sad incident and still remembers it to this day.

Keeping moose longer than a year, or even over winter, proved troublesome. Once grown, the moose could come and go over the cattle fencing at their leisure, but they also became somewhat of a nuisance at times, not wanting to leave when they should. If they wore out their welcome, they would need to be taken to another area, away from the rehab centre, for release back into their natural bush habitat.

Moose can be extremely dangerous, and although they do not have claws or canines, they will attack if provoked or if protecting their calf. When I say attack, I mean head down, ears back, full out charge until they reach you. Then they'll either trample you, if you have already assumed the fetal position on the ground, or knock you down with flailing karate-like front hooves, then proceed to use you like a dance floor and perform the Mexican two-step all over you. People have been killed this way by aggressive moose. In terms of sheer danger level to humans, I place them above a black bear and below a grizzly bear. So, getting between a moose cow and her calf is serious business. You'd best have eyes in the back of your head and a darn good pair of running shoes on if you're going to attempt it.

I had a neighbour back in '96 or '97 who was out for a spring walk and found a newborn calf entangled in a page-wire fence. Never giving the cow a thought, Jesse ambled over to the calf to try to help it. But when he heard the brush crashing behind him, he snapped his head up to see a cow moose boiling out of the bush and bearing down on him in a headlong charge. He turned and ran hard, managing to put about fifty yards between him and the calf before the cow caught up to him. Jesse showed me the scratches and bruises on his shoulders from where she had knocked him down by rearing up and striking him from behind. Fortunately, having put a little distance between himself and the calf, the cow's maternal instinct caused her to immediately leave him and run back to her calf, saving him from a thorough rototilling and serious injury.

I was always cautious dealing with moose, but I didn't think handling a set of easy-going twin calves that had been orphaned and rescued would be difficult. The twins, brother and sister, had grown to a weight of five or six hundred pounds each, and I wanted to relocate them together to an area south of Dawson Creek, way back in the boonies. I knew a friend with a four-horse stock trailer who was always eager to help me out with such things. I called him up and asked if he wanted to get into the moose moving business with me for a day. Without hesitation Doug agreed in his normal amicable manner, so we set a time to meet Leona at the rehab centre.

That early winter's day, the twins had been corralled in at the farmyard where a high-fenced cattle chute would help direct the moose into the stock trailer. Once the trailer was in place, we began gently shushing the moose down the chute toward the open trailer. A couple of heads of lettuce thrown onto the trailer floor really motivated the twins to get their front ends inside, but getting them to take that final step with their back legs up and onto the noisy trailer deck was a little more difficult.

The longer the process took, the closer we inched up behind the moose, not wanting to be the recipients of a nasty "cow-kick" in the you-know-whats. The twins seemed unimpressed and did not appear agitated by our presence behind them. All the while though, their necks were stretched out a mile trying in desperation to reach the tasty morsels of lettuce lying on the trailer floor just inches beyond the reach of their massively outstretched lips. While they were preoccupied, we slowly got close enough to lean our shoulders right into their hindquarters. Since the twins were now front-heavy from reaching in so far, we were able to quietly lift their hind feet off the ground and shove them into the trailer. Nary a hoof was flung, and the door was quietly slid shut behind them.

We were amazed by their calmness. I placed large brightly coloured ear tags on each twin, so the animals could be recognized if seen in the future. We then used the stock trailer's internal divider door to separate the moose to the front and back of the trailer, the brother in the front and sister in the rear. Standing behind the trailer, we gloated to each other and Leona over how easy the loading process had actually been, and that no doubt, we were professional moose whisperers.

Twin moose calves being relocated near
Dawson Creek after rehabilitation

The stock trailer rear door slid sideways and had a double latching mechanism that kept the door closed securely. To secure the door closed a top metal latch attached to the trailer body needed to be swung upward allowing the second latch (the door handle) to settle in behind a steel bar holding the door closed. Then the top latch would be swung down over the handle to keep it from popping up and releasing the door and could even be padlocked if desired. To re-open the door, the top latch had to be swung upward before the handle to open the door could be released. Although we did not lock it, it would still take those two actions and two hands to open the door. I remember to this day how Doug placed his hand on that mechanism, indicating it was securely in place and that we were ready to go. Still gloating to Leona over our victory, I agreed we should hit the road and get the twins moved.

We headed down the Old Hart Highway to where it joined Highway 97, hung a left at Arras onto the Tumbler Ridge Highway, and went all the way down to the Sundown Road, which accessed a multitude of old logging roads and cut blocks. Soon, we were into snow-covered side roads. Swapping tales and lies the entire way made the trip go by quickly. Before we knew it, we were in the middle of some old logging block in the middle of nowhere with timber nearby for cover: a perfect new home for the twins.

Exiting the passenger door and moving to the rear of the trailer I immediately saw there was a fairly serious problem. Somehow, the trailer door had slid open, and the rear stall was empty. I couldn't believe my eyes.

"Oh my God, Doug, we have a problem" were the only words I could muster.

Joining me at the rear of the trailer, "Holy shit" were the only words Doug could manage.

We both stood staring with our mouths dangling open. The sister was nowhere to be seen. This could not be real. It did not seem physically possible for that latch to have come open without help from the outside.

As we glanced back and forth at the open trailer and each other, our emotions quickly changed from disbelief to nervous laughter to utter horror. Perhaps she was lying injured or dead on the highway somewhere, complete with ear tags for easy identification. Or perhaps she was struck by a subsequent vehicle. Or maybe we caused an accident. Maybe we unknowingly left the scene of a horrific event that would undoubtedly make the headlines of the newspaper the next day. It was awful.

Over and over a variety of scenarios played out in my mind, none of which had a good or happy ending. The door had slid open to the "passenger" side of the trailer, so when by some stroke of magic the latch had come open, it was likely that a left-hand corner had probably helped the door slide to the side. Okay then, so the event most likely occurred on a hard left-hand corner, and the only such corner I could recall was where we had exited off Highway 97 onto the Tumbler Ridge Highway. Oh great, I envisioned her lying in the middle of the highway in Arras with a crowd of onlookers gathered around, flailing her broken legs in desperation, all the while showing off her ear tags, which everyone in the country would know the game warden had affixed. Great, just great.

Coming to the conclusion that there was absolutely nothing we could do in the present place or time to beam her back into the trailer, we begrudgingly started the process of releasing her brother. Fully opening the trailer doors, the young bull eagerly stepped down off the rear of the trailer, trotted off a distance, then stopped to look back, probably wondering where his lifelong partner had gone. I told the twin (in moose language of course) not to get himself shot during the next moose season. Then he wandered off alone, seemingly right at home in the bush.

Closing up the trailer, we were still confounded by how the latch had come open. So we blamed aliens, as there was absolutely no other way it could have happened. It was not humanly possible for that latch to open without outside help. It wasn't possible. Shaking our heads in disbelief, and totally deflated by the event, we began retracing our route, still blaming the aliens.

We cringed around every bend, expecting to see the sister lying in a crumpled heap as we continued to mull over all the scenarios and possible reasons for what had happened, all of which were nothing but theory. Then as we neared the Tumbler Ridge Highway on the snow and ice-covered Sundown Road, we noticed marks of some kind in the middle of the road. I asked Doug to stop the truck. After a quarter-mile or so on the slippery road, the truck and long trailer came to a sliding halt, and I bailed out of the truck. Running back, I could see two distinct drag marks about two feet apart on the hard-packed snow going right down the middle of the road. Following the marks back for about a hundred yards, I could see they abruptly ended where a big disturbance in the snow indicated something had rolled into the ditch. From there, big, healthy moose tracks trotted up the ditch line for about fifty yards, then left the road and entered the bush. Following the running moose tracks for a distance, I could see that a moose had left the scene on four healthy and unbroken legs. There was no blood or any tufts of moose hair.

It was clear to us now. When the aliens had unlatched the door of the moving trailer, the door began jiggling and sliding sideways. All the while the two dummies in the front seat were blissfully ignorant of the drama unfolding at the rear of the stock trailer behind them. From the marks on the road, it appeared that she had attempted to step out of the trailer when the door slid open enough to allow for her escape. As both her front feet were planted on the road, which was moving away from her at thirty kilometres per hour, she had gone down onto her chest with her hind end still firmly planted in the trailer. As her front end was being dragged along the road backwards, her front hooves left the distinct drag marks down the middle of the road. Finally, probably due to sheer panic and outright flailing, the twin popped out of the back of the trailer, did a couple of 360-degree spins on her way to the ditch, flailed around a bit, gathered up her legs and took off like the wind.

Hooray! No dead or injured moose, no vehicle collisions, no headlines and most importantly no witnesses! It appeared that the young cow had made it through the escape unharmed. Unfortunately, she was not released with her brother, but at least it seemed she was okay. The icy road had really helped her in that regard. Had the road been dry gravel, there would have been some serious road rash. Relieved, Doug and I both laughed hard about the entire event, and how it had all played out. We swore each other to secrecy and that aliens were to blame, and that no one, especially Leona, could ever know about us losing the moose.

Sorry, Doug, enough time has passed; it's time people knew that aliens actually do lurk out there in our forests!

2

A VERY BIG
BRUIN

A resident of the Upper Pemberton Valley had the living daylights spooked out of him when he inadvertently bumped into a large grizzly bear while cutting cedar shakes. The incident occurred on a large piece of private land where the owner had earlier butchered a cow and placed the remains on the rear side of the property for the ravens and coyotes to clean up. Although grizzlies were not that common in the area, there had been occasional sightings and encounters. Odours from animal carcass remains will attract a grizzly bear from a long distance. They can't resist the smell of decaying meat and are very aggressive when encountered at an animal kill they have made or at carcass remains. More than one person has been mauled or killed this way.

We got the call at our Squamish CO office, and the next day my partners Paul, Shawn and I headed up to check out the complaint. The landowner met us and took us up to the site where the bear had been encountered. We very cautiously entered the area and located the carcass remains. It was evident from the horse-sized manure piles that a very large grizzly had been feeding on the remains. Though the bear really hadn't done anything wrong up to that point, there were farms and families in the area. We thought it best to try to catch the bear and move it out of the area to prevent any further human interactions, which might go badly. Using the few bits of beef remains as well as some rotten salmon we had brought along, I set a cable leg snare in amongst the large cedar trees in an attempt to live capture the bear. We finished up the snare set as best we could then headed for home. We would check the snare first thing in the morning.

A leg snare consists of a length of 3/16-inch or 1/4-inch steel cable fashioned into a sliding loop with a one-way sliding lock on one end (the business end), and a small fixed loop on the other end (the anchoring end). The cable is looped through itself around an anchor, in this case a large cedar tree, and the snare loop is laid over a spring-triggering mechanism. Bait is placed beyond the snare, at the rear of a three-foot brush enclosure open at the front (a cubby). The front opening directs the bear toward the bait. Unless previously captured in a snare, a bear (or cougar) will usually take the most direct route to the bait and enter through the front opening. The bear will lift its front foot over a strategically placed step log and step onto the hidden spring trigger, which releases the spring and sends the cable loop up around the leg above the paw. The one-way sliding lock enables the loop to tighten around the bear's leg when it attempts to step away but does not allow the loop to loosen. While some bears do not fight the cable at all, most will resist it for a while, then lie quietly once they tire. By their nature though, grizzly bears tend to fight a leg snare more aggressively than other bears, so it is imperative to check a grizzly snare as soon as possible.

Paul, Shawn and I headed up early the next day in anticipation of what might lie ahead of us. Working with grizzlies was always exciting as we didn't deal with very many in the Lower Mainland area. When we arrived, the landowner advised us there was indeed a bear in the snare, so I parked the truck nearby to prepare the tranquillizing equipment. The guys wanted to go in and get a look at the bear, but not knowing the condition of the snare cable I advised against it. We had no idea when the bear had been caught, and grizzlies often gnaw at the steel cable. This was always a serious concern because, unlike black bears, a snared grizzly will invariably charge when approached. I had been told about instances when a severely chewed snare cable had snapped when a bear charged, and bad things had happened. As such, I never approached a snared grizzly on foot if there was another alternative. But the guys were adamant and decided to walk in the last 100 yards to get a look anyway. About thirty seconds later they hot-footed it back out, moving a lot faster than they went in. The bear had indeed charged. Fortunately for them, the cable had held.

After the tranquillizing and safety equipment was ready to go, I slowly drove the truck to within decent darting range of the bear, about thirty yards. I was fairly shocked to see the size of the grizzly. It was big. Paul readied the tranquillizing gun from the safety of the truck, and when the bear stepped into the open from behind the big cedar, Paul got the first dart into the big bear's hip muscle. The bear would not go down easy, so he had to put two more darts into it before we could approach.

The grizzly was beautiful. It was a large boar (male), and it was all we could do to get him rolled into a position to remove the snare. His head was massive. By far the biggest bear I had ever dealt with up to that time. He was an honest eight-footer, head to tail. I could not estimate his weight though; he was simply too big.

Our culvert bear trap was presently in use at another complaint, so we asked the area park rangers if we could borrow theirs to move the bear. Their trap was slightly smaller than ours, but we thought it would work fine. It would take a couple of hours to get their trap, so we needed to secure the bear until then; we sure didn't need the big guy coming out his drug-induced sleep while unsecured. We also didn't want him fighting a single snare on one leg either. We had a number of snares with us, so we proned out the big grizzly with four snares between the landowner's tractor and a large cedar tree.

Culvert traps are just that; an eight-foot length of four-foot diameter steel culvert with a hinged sprung door at one end and a heavy steel mesh screening on the other end. A trigger mechanism holds the door open until bait hung at the front of the trap is pulled, releasing the door. Hinged with a heavy spring, the door quickly slams shut, locking the bear inside. In this case, though, we just needed a culvert trap to hold and safely transport the bear.

In a couple of hours we had the Parks bear trap, and Dennis, the Predator Control Officer for the Lower Mainland, came up to lend his bear expertise. The big bruin had come out of the drug by this time and was quietly laying with his head up. We did not know what the bear weighed, but it was very heavy, and we knew we could never pull him into the trap by hand once he was drugged again. Therefore, we ran a winch cable from the truck through the steel grating on the front of the live trap and out through the back door. Then we drugged the grizzly again. Once more, it fought the drug and it took additional doses to put him completely out. I was worried that we might overdose him, as I had never used so much drug on a bear before. But then again, I had never dealt with a bear with so much body mass.

Once immobilized, we worked quickly to affix a small ear tag and remove the restraining snares from his legs. We then rigged a large set of handcuffs to his rear legs to which we could attach the winch cable. Fortunately, the Parks' live trap had a ramp at the door, so we began to winch the big guy up into the trap by his back feet. He slid up the ramp on his stomach very nicely, and soon his huge bulk filled up the bottom two-thirds of the forty-inch-tall trap door. There was an issue though; the trap was eight feet long, and when his body slid into the trap and his hind feet touched the far end, his head, shoulders and front legs were still lying outside the door on the ramp. He was that big. Additionally, someone was going to have to climb inside the trap and remove the rear leg shackles and winch line.

Paul and Shawn were still a little puckered from their earlier interaction with the grizzly, so I got elected for the job. There was no time to stand around talking about it, so I went in while Paul stood at the bear's head with a shotgun in case of trouble. With the grizzly's huge prone body taking up the majority of the door opening, I had to crawl up over his head and shoulders to get into the trap to get to his rear feet at the far end. Once inside, I tried to ignore the intimidation factor and worked as fast as I could to remove the hardware on his legs. I had handled dozens of drugged bears previously and knew I was safe, but it was still intimidating. Suddenly I heard, "Keith, his head's up."

Turning around I saw the big bear had his head upright, looking away from me. I knew he was still very groggy, but nothing makes a guy work faster than having a semi-awake eight-foot, massive grizzly bear lying between him and the only way out!

Having personally experienced the jaws of a much smaller female (sow) grizzly in Bella Coola in 1987 (more on that later), I was fully aware of the capabilities of this big bear and wanted no part of his business end. Thankfully, having drugged many bears previously, I knew how they behaved when coming out of the drug. I felt my peril wasn't too terribly grievous at this point and told Paul to hold off with the shotgun. I quickly turned back and focused on the job of removing the shackles and winch line. Then, Ninja-style, I launched myself over the bear's shoulders and head and out the door. I don't know how I flew out the small gap above the bear's shoulders without cracking my skull on the metal door frame, but I got out, and fast. Safely out, the bear had now lowered his head again. We lifted his massive forelegs and pushed them into the trap on either side of the door. Then we pushed his head and shoulders into the trap the best we could, making sure he was able to breathe freely, covered his eyes and closed the door. He was safely in, and we all breathed a heavy sigh of relief together.

Keith with secured boar grizzly before it was
winched into a live trap for relocation

Now we had another problem, the huge bear's weight had flattened the trap tires. We managed to locate a bicycle hand pump somewhere, solved that problem, and soon we were ready to head out.

Grizzly bears are notorious for travelling long distances to return to their home range when relocated. A helicopter is the preferred mode of travel for relocation; however, helicopter dollars were lean at the time. Our only choice was to take him as far away from human activity as possible via road. I hoped his negative snare experience with humans might keep him away from other human activity and out of trouble, at least for a while.

We drove fifty kilometres to an old logging landing, which was not far enough away for a grizzly, but the choices for truly remote relocation sites in the interior were few. We did the best we could in finding a location as far away from any residences and people as possible.

In preparation for the release, we set up a stick man with work coveralls away from the trap to divert his attention away from us and the trucks. Released grizzlies have been known to turn their natural aggressive tendencies loose on a truck on more than one occasion. They will often charge at anything in sight when released, including biting and flattening truck tires and ripping mirrors off, so we hoped to divert his attention. I recalled watching and listening to a video taken by a fellow CO while releasing a grizzly, and how his calm, professional narrating voice went up about ten octaves when the bear charged his truck. His 4x4 tires could be heard blowing as the bear unleashed his aggression on them.

Paul and Dennis were together in one truck, and they parked behind the trap at the far end of the landing in order to handle the long rope attached to the door release. Our plan was to let the stick man handle the initial diversion when the door was released, then hope the bear would simply opt to leave the site without further aggression toward us or our vehicles.

As the door was pulled open, the big grizzly came out like a half-ton bull and flattened the stickman. Though he was still slightly under the effect of the drug, he was plenty capable of causing serious damage. He lay on the mangled stick man for a short time probably expecting a struggle. He then turned and charged my truck when we hollered at him to leave. Shawn and I were standing on my truck's running boards but quickly piled into the truck and pulled it forward a safe distance when the charge began. The only thing slowing the bear down was the remnants of the drug at this point, so he lay down, then promptly charged us a second time. Once again, I jumped in and pulled the truck forward away from the bear.

With twenty-twenty hindsight, we realized the placement of Dennis's truck hadn't been the greatest. I was parked in front of the bear and could drive my truck out of the landing, but we now had to get Dennis's truck out from the rear of the landing in order to give the bear room to make its exit. The big grizzly was now blocking Dennis' exit though. Without hesitation, Dennis put his Suburban in gear and floored it past the grizzly and toward us. Paul was on the passenger side, and as the truck passed, the grizzly reared up and lunged at that side of the truck. Well, I'm sure I saw Paul go airborne and leap right across the front seat darn near onto Dennis's lap. Once past though, the bear lay back down again and surveyed the area for other targets to take his aggression out on. We stood quietly with nervous grins on our faces. Finally, the bear stood up and sauntered off the rear of the landing and into the bush, past where Dennis's truck had been parked. It had been quite a bear experience, and we were happy the big grizzly was away from humans, for now.

After I transferred to Dawson Creek the big grizzly was caught a second time in the area and was recognized by the ear tag. This time he was relocated far away to the outer coast by helicopter. The pilot knew his chopper's lifting capabilities well, as all helicopter pilots do, and advised the bear was pushing a thousand pounds.

3

POTATO RODEO

Over the years growing up near Kamloops, British Columbia, our family owned horses and also boarded a few. When I was quite young, we lived at the edge of Valleyview and had enough property to keep one horse. Then, by the time I was about ten years old, we got our first horse. It was my sister Denise's horse. She loved Misty, but he was a devious dapple-grey gelding that I never really trusted. Mom and Dad had a big garden, and Dad built a root cellar out in the middle of the pasture for cold storage. Every time Mom needed carrots for supper, it seemed I was the lucky one who had to venture through the pasture where Misty lurked. I had to outsmart and outrun that nag or he would physically harass me into dropping my load of carrots as I ran for the for the safety of the fence.

Eventually, we moved out of town and built a home on an acreage where we constructed a good-sized barn and a hay shed for several horses. I spent my time hauling hay, trimming hooves and shoveling horse manure for many years. Those experiences growing up taught me a lot about horses and their behaviour.

In the fall of 1984, Jim, the Quesnel CO, planned to make an enforcement patrol by horseback for caribou hunters into the Itcha Mountains that lie just north of Nimpo Lake in the Cariboo.

My hand went up right away and plans were made for the trip. Although I had no pack train experience, I figured my time spent around horses would hopefully be an asset.

Keith and pack train into Itcha Mountains

As I prepared for the pack trip, I recalled a hunter check I did involving horses in 1983. It was still clear in my mind. Myself and Bob, a Kamloops-based CO, were checking the Lillooet backcountry for a few days, and we ended up in Relay Creek. High country mule deer and sheep hunters used the area. We spent the night camped out in the rear of the truck. Late in the day, a pair of sheep hunters came past our parking spot on horseback, each trailing a packhorse. I noticed the height of the loads on their two pack horses and mentioned to Bob that the volume of gear loaded on their horses seemed a little extreme. We briefly talked with the riders and wished them well. They rode on past us eager to get to their first camp spot.

After a tailgate breakfast the next morning, we bounced our way up to the end of the boulder-infested mining road and found a couple of hunter camps, one of which belonged to the horseback hunters. It was nine in the morning by this point, and the two riders had just finished breaking camp, loading their pack horses, and were just preparing to mount up and head up the trail. Their bright red plywood panniers (pack boxes) looked spiffy and were brand new, and once again I noticed the over-height loads as they covered the colourful new panniers with tarps and tied their last diamond hitch. I was no horseman, but their loads looked awfully top-heavy and might be prone to slipping and rolling on the horses. It was clear by the amount of gear that these guys intended to have a really comfortable hunting camp, with lots of grub for the duration.

The first of the two riders mounted his saddle horse and led his packhorse to the edge of the camp where the trail immediately led up a steep hill. He stopped and waited for his partner to mount up, but his packhorse began getting anxious and was side-stepping. This was typical of a horse "feeling its oats" at the start of a day trip. As the second hunter finally untied his saddle horse from the rail and threw his leg over the saddle, his partner could no longer wait with his fidgeting packhorse and started leading it up the steep trail.

Fifty feet up the hill the big packhorse began balking and quickly jerked the lead rope from the rider's hand. As we and his partner watched wide-eyed from the camp, his packhorse turned around and charged headlong down the trail back toward camp. About three jumps into the downhill gallop, the top-heavy bouncing pack slipped and rolled under the horse. Now things got really interesting. That gelding went into a wild bucking fit and plunged down the hill, smashing those nice new panniers to smithereens. There were chunks of red plywood, carrots, spuds, onions, pots and pans flying in all directions. The load was now a smashed pile of debris flopping and dragging under the horse. The slack cinch and diamond hitch then slid back to its flanks and rear legs, and the bucking became frantic until the last of the pack remnants were mutilated and kicked off in a heap at the trailhead.

His partner sat on his horse watching the entire event, then slowly brought his leg back over the saddle and simply re-tied his horses. We stood there stunned along with his partner and did our very best to choke back a nervous laugh. We were relieved though that the horse and rider were not injured. I felt bad for them, as that was the extent of their pack trip for that particular day. We left them trying to sort out their gear and predicament, and I don't know if they ever did get their new red panniers re-built or their horses into the mountains.

The vision of airborne potatoes, carrots, pots, pans and pieces of panniers was still fresh in my mind as we loaded our horses for the week-long pack trip into the Itcha Mountains. We had four horses: two saddle horses and two packhorses. Two of the horses were Jim's, and the other two horses belonged to a local wildlife biologist. Jim had done pack trips previously and knew how to properly load, weigh and tie the packs on the horses. I really enjoyed learning about it and quickly learned the tricks of loading and tying pack horses. We drove to the trailhead west of Nazko, unloaded the horses and headed west toward the Itchas on a cut line.

Jim and I rode the two best saddle horses, and we each led a packhorse. I rode a nice solid grey mare with a great disposition and led a big grey gelding, not unlike old Misty. The gelding was pretty fat and had no withers for the pack saddle to settle on; I was worried that if he got too sweaty his load might slip, even though we kept the load height and weight to a minimum. But he needed the exercise, so he got to wear the load. Jim's packhorse was a little on the heavy side too.

We had a twenty-five-mile ride ahead of us, and we planned to do it over two days. So off we rode. All went well until we hit a boggy stretch, where the mud was almost belly deep, and my big grey pack gelding was struggling to get through. Jim was in the lead and had cleared the bog when the big grey just stopped. Turning around, I could see his load had slipped on him and rolled under him, but being tired, he just stood his ground. Alright! No potato rodeo for this guy today! He patiently stood quietly as we untied his pack. Then we re-packed the load on my mare, which had a great set of withers for better pack stability. We carried on without incident, but the big gelding was a lot less comfortable to ride due to his width.

I've never been a very trusting soul around horses, as given half the chance, they will get you into trouble if the opportunity presents itself. On more than one occasion while growing up I'd had a horse buck me off and head for home on a dead run. I wasn't about to give these horses the chance to do the same. So, I made a dedicated habit of always tying the horses when we stopped and got off them. However, as we neared the end of our first day's ride toward our camp, I was getting more comfortable and trusting with the horses and began not to tie the gelding when stopping for a break. I did keep the pack mare tied to my saddle horn though. The farther we got from the truck, the less interested they seemed in heading home. Also, the two sets of horses were buddies from their own home pastures and that helped. As mentioned, it was all good, sort of, until the two sets of buddies got separated.

On day two I was riding the mare again for comfort, and the fat gelding carried the pack. Our destination was a Ski-Doo cabin on the east flank of the Itcha Mountains, but Jim didn't exactly know where it was. We were looking for a dim trail that led south, but nothing stood out. The trail had petered out and the bush was getting thick, so we stopped and let the horses crop a bit of meadow grass. We had dropped their reins, but I stood with the horses while Jim walked on ahead a short distance to see if he could find the trail. He figured we had ridden past it. Jim's horses were up the trail in front of mine, and he got back to them before I got to mine. He stepped into the saddle and turned his horses back the way we had come, so my saddle horse figured it was time to go. She turned to leave without me, with the gelding tied to the saddle horn.

There she went, casually leading my packhorse back down the trail out in front of me behind Jim. I let out a gentle, "Whoa," not wanting to spook them by hollering or running. I just quick-stepped alongside my pack horse's flank, as the mare began to walk faster down the trail toward home following Jim's horses. We had gone about twenty feet and being out front Jim hadn't seen my predicament, yet I could see where this story was heading, so I made one desperate lunge to grab the gelding's lead rope. The knot came off the saddle horn and the mare took that as a starting gun. The gelding stopped because I held his lead rope, but the mare was off and running down the trail like a cut cat with stirrups flopping on both sides. At a full gallop, she quickly disappeared past Jim. I knew I had made a mistake dropping her reins about the time Jim had stepped into the saddle. I had my rifle along for bear protection and knew that the weight of it on one side would roll the saddle. Once that happened with her galloping, I envisioned my rifle stock getting smashed off behind the trigger, and the saddle cinch snapping. Lovely!

Jim agreed to go after her, so I held both pack horses on foot, while he galloped off to find her. We had no idea how far he would have to ride to catch her, and if the saddle didn't roll and stop her, she could go a long way toward home.

Now I stood on foot with two loaded pack horses whose buddies had disappeared down the trail, and heaven forbid they should be without their pals. The whinnying and side-stepping show started, and I fought to control them by their lead ropes. I should have tied them right then and there, but I told him I would walk the horses back and try to find the trail to the cabin. Now I was leading them down the middle of a large moose meadow with no trees within a hundred feet to tie to. The horses continued to whinny for their buddies until suddenly they just stopped and stood their ground behind me. Just like the day before, I turned around to see the grey had slipped its load again. It had gone down on one knee from the shifted weight lying under its belly.

It was a good thing my rifle was on my missing saddle horse and that my pistol was buried in my pack, or I might have sent that packhorse to the big pasture in the sky. All the premonitions about the trouble that horses can get a person into were becoming real!

With no trees to tie to, one horse down, and one horse doing a side-stepping "missing his buddy" routine, I started to remove the slipped pack with one hand while holding on the lead ropes with the other. I called those horses every name in the frikkin' book, but somehow, over a ten-minute period, I managed to get the pack to drop to the ground while not losing either horse. About that time Jim came trotting back with my saddle horse, with everything including my rifle intact. She had run about a mile down the trail until the saddle rolled, then had stood her ground. Thankfully she must have stopped right away, saving my rifle stock, the saddle and its rigging from being damaged. And it turned out the cabin was only a few hundred yards from where the pack rolled.

Fortunately, we got all those bugs worked out on the front end of the trip and had no other incidents the entire week. We made our patrols on the saddle horses, covering lots of ground looking for caribou hunters, leaving the other two horses to keep each other company back at the cabin. We checked a few hunters who were very surprised to meet us in the mountains, saw some beautiful alpine country, and really enjoyed the trip. But as much as I like being around them, I still don't completely trust horses.

4

PREDATOR

It was a pleasant summer morning in 2001, and I was enjoying a coffee at home in Hagensborg, watching a colourful rufous hummingbird above the back deck at the feeder. He would enjoy a sip, fly away twenty feet to where he would make his springtime mating display, then return to the feeder. He repeated this process for several minutes, all the while trying to ward off any other males vying for a drink at the feeder. That little hummingbird was a really busy guy, and he started making me feel just a bit guilty for sitting and drinking coffee. Then the phone rang.

A lady was calling to report that she had just seen a cougar beside her chicken coop close to her home. Her property was just across the Bella Coola River from where we lived at the time, so I deserted my coffee and fired up the truck to make the quick drive over. Once there she explained that the cat had left just moments before my arrival. The timber was quite dense behind her home, so I figured the cougar had probably gone that direction and disappeared into the bush. The cougar had only made an appearance and had not attacked any of her animals, so I decided not to take any action and advised her to keep a keen eye out in case it reappeared. I told her to call me right away again if it did come back. She understood and thanked me for coming over. Although I had taken no action at that point, I was concerned about the proximity of other homes and residents nearby.

An hour later that same pot of coffee was still tasting pretty nice as I continued to watch the little hummingbird. Then, the phone rang again. The caller this time, Jack, lived close to where the earlier cougar sighting had occurred. He stated he was presently standing at his living room window looking at a cougar standing in his garden. I told him there had been another cougar call earlier that morning from his close neighbour, so it was likely the same cougar. I said I'd be right over.

Jumping into the truck, I made a quick left onto the highway, then a quick right onto Saloompt Road toward Jack's place. Motoring down the straight stretch toward Jack's, I glanced in my rearview mirror and saw what looked like a blizzard behind me. At first, it didn't register with me what was happening, then it hit me. Oh no, Paul's prank!

Pulling a good prank has always been something I've enjoyed doing, and my colleague Paul felt the same way. Earlier that year, I had removed the driver's seat from his brand-new patrol vehicle while he was away on holidays and replaced it with an unused outhouse toilet I had borrowed from the BC Parks' warehouse. In retaliation, Paul had filled the cab of my patrol vehicle with styrofoam packing peanuts. Every nook and cranny right to the window line inside the cab was filled with those nasty little tidbits that clung to everything. Shannon was standing beside me and howled with laughter when I opened the driver's door and an avalanche came pouring out. I just shook my head …Well played, Paul. If you've ever tried, it is impossible to sweep those little suckers up. Therefore the big Shop-Vac got put to good use, and I filled it to the brim.

I had set the full Shop-Vac in the rear of my work truck after attending the initial cougar call that morning, as I was planning on stopping at the landfill later that day on my way to the office.

That was when Jack had called and that plan got put on hold. Now, motoring toward Jack's I realized the Shop-Vac had flipped onto its side during the hard S-turn and the lid had popped off. The wind was carrying the contents out and onto the road like a raging January snowstorm behind me. All I could do was shake my head in disbelief and carry on. I'd have to come back later and clean it up. The cougar call was the top priority.

Arriving at Jack's, he quickly relayed the events, stating the cat had slowly sauntered off and out of sight around the back of the house. It seemed this cougar was intent on hanging around residences. My first concern was for the many homes in the area that had small children. I always made a point of trying to leave animals alone if they were passing through, but the last thing I wanted was a cougar attacking a child. So I thought I'd best try to find the cat.

Jack and I surveyed the tracks left behind in the garden's soft soil, confirming the cougar had gone the direction Jack had indicated. There was fairly dense bush at the edge of the yard, which would provide good cover for a cougar, and we could hear a squirrel that was agitated, chattering about fifty metres away from us in the bush: a result of the large cat being present I presumed.

I carried my trusty work .30-06 rifle on this occasion, as it performed well when dealing with these sorts of calls. Unfortunately for the cougar, I needed to draw the animal out into the open for a clear shot. Typically, a cougar reacts to a predator call, which resembles the sound of a distressed rabbit, however in my haste I had left the house without my predator calls. Therefore I positioned Jack in a safe spot on the porch and told him to stand quietly for a few minutes. A short distance away I knelt down where I had a rest for my rifle and began to squeak as loud as I could with my lips to imitate a predator call.

About ten minutes passed and the cat didn't show itself. Jack and I shrugged our shoulders and quietly walked back around the corner of the house, past two garden sheds, and back to the far side of the garden. Standing on the lawn at the edge of the raspberry cane rows we discussed our next move. Suddenly, a tapping noise at the house forty metres away caught my attention. Inside the large living room window was Jack's wife frantically knocking on the window and pointing back to where we had just walked. Stepping out past the edge of the tall raspberry canes that blocked our view, I could see what she was frantically pointing at—an adult cougar standing on the lawn. It was twenty metres from us and was standing in front of the sheds we had just walked past thirty seconds ago. The cougar must have been between the two sheds, or mighty close to them when we passed. It had been coming in to investigate my squealing after all.

Jack was just to my right and could not see the cougar around the tall raspberry canes, so I immediately blurted, "There's the cougar, Jack!" The very instant the cat and I made eye contact it turned and slipped into the raspberries. Jack's garden was meticulous. The rows of raspberry canes were completely weed-free, creating immaculate dirt tunnels between them. The cougar slipped past the first row of raspberries and into the tunnel, which by chance ended right at our feet. The cougar then turned toward Jack and me and quickly began slinking toward us in predator mode along the tunnel. This was happening fast, and I could see it coming through the tunnel. Jack however still did not realize what was happening, so I reached across his chest with my right arm and told him, "Get back, get back!" while stepping rearward and pushing him back at the same time. I put about eight feet between us and the edge of the garden. Then as the cougar reached the end of the tunnel at the garden's edge it stopped and peered out at us in a low crouched position, gathering up its rear legs and switching its tail. I was in disbelief at what I was seeing—a cougar stalking two grown adults. As it stopped at the end of the tunnel, crouched and glared at me, I shouldered my .30-06 and fired, instantly killing the big cat.

Keith with the male cougar that stalked him and a
property owner to within point-blank range

Jack hadn't seen the cougar until its head had protruded
from the raspberries, and then I had fired my loud rifle at that
moment, so he was pretty startled by the whole event. From
the time I made eye contact with the cougar until I shot it was
probably less than ten seconds. We both stood there in disbelief.
It was a remarkable lesson on how easy it is for cougars to be
nearby while not being seen. After, Jack commented a number of
times how he had been in the garden all morning working with
his head down pulling weeds, and I know that caused him some
real concern after the fact.

The cougar was an averaged sized male in good health, and it
was unfortunate that it had to be destroyed. However, the cougar's
intentions were fairly clear when it pulled itself up into a predatory
crouch at our feet. Its actions spoke volumes.

5

JUSTICE

Most angler checks ended with nothing more than pleasant conversation, however, at times some did not follow that script. One early August day, I drove up the Sea to Sky Highway toward Whistler from Squamish and noticed a van parked at a bridge where a forest service road crossed the Cheakamus River.

The Cheakamus flowed out of Daisy Lake and was a fast, rumbling and bouldery river. There wasn't a lot of slow-moving water in this upper stretch of river where the fish could hold, and the fish tended to be quite small. It was actually hard to find any rainbow trout in this part of the river that were over the thirty centimetre (12 inch) minimum size limit. The best water to fish at this location was a slower pool right under the bridge. Having checked anglers here previously, I parked short of the bridge and walked past the parked van, which appeared empty.

On the bridge, I peered over the side and could see a lone, middle-aged man about twenty feet below at the river's edge, bent over gathering up his fishing rod and creel. The river's roar was loud, so trying to speak to him from above was not possible. As I stood thinking of what to do, he began to walk up the trail toward the road with his gear. Walking back along the road I

31

paralleled his trail, and soon the man's bobbing head appeared as he gained elevation, making his way toward the road where I was standing. At this point, the trail was still thirty feet from me, with a few willow saplings between me and the angler. As he walked along, he looked over and saw me waiting in full uniform at the road edge and immediately stopped. Without hesitation, he bent over, disappearing for a few seconds, then straightened up and continued to walk up the trail toward me. Interesting. Now my CO senses were fired up and working.

As he reached where I stood, I noticed right away that he was not carrying the creel. Starting the check, we had a pleasant enough conversation, and I asked for his fishing licence which was all good. When I asked how the fishing had been, he said he had not caught anything. I asked him where the creel was he had just been carrying. He shrugged and said he didn't know what I was talking about. Oh great, here we go, my built-in lie detector was kicking in now. Well, we went back and forth about the creel for a minute, and he maintained he did not have one. Seeing I was getting nowhere with him, I hurried down the trail and found the creel sitting beside the trail where he had stopped and put it down. Picking it up and walking back, he continued to deny the creel was his. Opening it, there were at least a dozen small rainbow trout, all of which were undersize, with some being no bigger than three or four inches long.

It became apparent that he was not going to admit the creel and fish were his, and he continued lying profusely. Therefore the discussion with him ended, and I began writing him up for both the over-limit and undersized trout. Checking his fishing gear, it too was illegal. Being that he had killed a dozen illegal rainbow trout with illegal gear, in addition to not owning up to the deed, he was going to get the preverbal book thrown at him. He became incredulous, and soon began pleading with me to give him "a break." I explained to him how what he had done was illegal on all fronts, and he had also lied to me, so no, he would be getting no breaks.

Creel of undersized rainbow trout caught in the Cheakamus River. Note shotgun shell placed alongside for size comparison

The man kept pleading with me to stop writing him up. Then suddenly, in his European accent, he stated, "OK, if you no give me a break, I lie in court, and you attack my wife." The man's heavy accent made it difficult to understand, but I got the gist of it, so I asked him to repeat what he had said. Again, he said, "You no give me a break, you attack my wife." I was astounded by his statement, and the threatening accusation was filtering its way into my little pea brain. So, I asked him where this wife of his was that he was accusing me of attacking. He motioned with his hand toward the van. I walked over to it and sure enough, now there was a woman sitting in the passenger seat. She must have been out of sight in the rear of the van when I had walked past previously. Then he changed his story and stated she had caught a number of the fish as well as him. I got the two separated and immediately asked her if she had caught any fish. She said she had not, and having been in the van she was unaware of how her husband's fishing had been, or that I had caught him with a bag full of illegal trout.

Rarely over the years did I outwardly get upset at someone I encountered, but as the minutes ticked by, I found myself getting very upset and had to hold myself back from saying something I would regret as a professional. Advising him that he was terribly out of line with his comments, I seized all his fishing gear, served him his ticket and walked to my truck to get my camera. I then photographed the van and creel of fish. From there I drove straight to the RCMP detachment in Squamish and reported the incident, in the event the man took it upon himself to falsify a complaint about me to the police.

I was somewhat pleased when he later disputed the ticket fines, and the case went right to a Provincial Court trial. On the witness stand, I relayed all the details of our entire creek-side conversation, which included how the so-called angler had accused me of attacking his wife once I had begun writing him a ticket. My photograph of the creel filled with tiny rainbow trout was also entered as evidence and sealed the verdict. I took great satisfaction in hearing the judge find the lying fish poacher guilty on all counts, levy a heavier fine than the ticketed amount, and give him a severe verbal undressing for his pathetic words and actions as a resource abuser that day. In the end, had the man recognized his wrongdoing and simply paid his ticketed fines he would have saved himself a heavier fine, as well as a fair bit of public humiliation. Justice served.

6

WALKABOUT

Over the years in Dawson Creek, I had heard a few reports about mountain wildlife species appearing and passing through the agriculture farmland areas. There were bonafide sightings of stone sheep near Chetwynd and mountain goats on the bluffs where Highway 97 crosses the Kiskatinaw River, just north of town. Being that Dawson Creek is not too far as the crow flies from the mountain country of Tumbler Ridge, it was possible for mountain wildlife to go on a walkabout every so often to check out a new range. After all, that is how many wildlife species arrived in North America, via the land bridge that existed between Russia and Alaska 16,000 years ago.

Our home was located in Arras not far from Highway 52, the Tumbler Ridge Highway. The area was undulating rolling hills, with many farm fields producing annual seed crops and hay. It was not the type of country you would expect to see an animal that normally resided in the Rocky Mountains. That is why I was more than a little dubious when my next-door neighbour called me at the office one summer day in 1995 and told me that a mountain goat was perched on her doorstep.

First, she asked me what mountain goats looked like, so I explained that they were white with short, curved black horns.

She said it was white, but that the horns were blackish-brown. The bottom portion of mountain goat horns do have a bit of dark brown colouring, so I supposed it was possible it was a mountain goat. I asked her if perhaps it was a domestic goat, but she did not think so as she had owned goats previously. By the end of the call, I was very interested in what might be standing on her porch. I told her that I'd come out and have a look.

Just in case the critter actually turned out to be a mountain goat or some other animal I needed to deal with, I wanted to be prepared. So I gathered up my tranquillizing equipment and also hitched up the culvert bear trap to serve as a portable holding facility.

Pulling into my neighbour's farmyard on their quarter section, my eyes bugged out when I spotted an Oreamnos americanus standing on their deck: an actual mountain goat … a young billy (a male). I was fairly shocked, to say the least. The low-lying deck was large and located at the front of the house. The billy was standing with its rump backed up against the screen door and had an expression that indicated he was not planning on going anywhere soon. A couple of their dogs were barking at it from the base of the stairs, but the billy was intentionally ignoring them. It was apparent that the goat had taken refuge on the deck to get away from the dogs (and also the dogs had taken refuge from the goat down on the ground). Like any wild animal, goats can be dangerous at close range and will lower their head and slash upward if threatened at close quarters.

The property sat only 32 kilometres east of the Murray River, where I had personally seen mountain goats in a side-drainage while elk hunting a few years earlier. The Murray River parallels the east flank of the mountains, not far from goat country.

Mountain goats do go on occasional walkabouts. I had once seen photographs of a mountain goat swimming across Hotnarko Lake in the West Chilcotin area, quite a distance from any mountains. I also recalled how in the seventies Dad and I were deer hunting in the Falkland area. A fellow who was manning a fire lookout tower told us about a billy goat that had shown up out of nowhere, hung around for a few days, then simply moved on. Although I was surprised the goat on the deck had arrived in the area, it certainly was close enough to the Murray River to have travelled overland from there.

Mountain goat backed onto porch by dogs in
Dawson Creek farm country prior to being relocated
to mountain country near Tumbler Ridge

My neighbour advised that she had been unaware the goat was on the deck until a BC Hydro employee had pulled into the yard to read the meter. She owned a number of dogs, one of which I believe was a large white long-haired Maremma sheepdog. Anyway, it was big and white, and the meter reader had been greeted many times by the dog. The hydro meter was located on the side of the house above the deck, and this day was no different than any other meter-reading day. The meter reader was well up onto the deck before he realized the big white dog standing on the deck was actually a big white mountain goat. The goat stomped a front hoof in a display of stress-induced aggression, lowered its head and charged across the deck at him. The meter reader aborted his mission with one airborne leap, and quickly retreated to the safety of his vehicle. The goat then firmly replanted its hindquarters against the screen door, where it knew its back end was not exposed to the dogs, and stood its ground.

As I approached the deck, the billy lowered its head and stomped a front hoof to warn me that I was getting too close to him. Goat horns are sharp and very capable of inflicting serious injury, and I did not want to risk having one of those stuck in my butt (or worse), so I backed off. I kept experimenting with the distance until I found the closest point where he would tolerate my presence, then I stuck a dart full of Telezol in him.

Telezol is a mixed drug that works well on bears, but only performs marginally on ungulates and other hoofed animals. As such, it took two good-sized darts to put the billy down, and even then, he wasn't sleeping as soundly as I normally preferred with bears and moose. Nonetheless, I got him ear-tagged and loaded into the bear trap without incident, and with a goodbye headed to higher ground.

Just over an hour later, south of Tumbler Ridge on top of Quintette Mountain in the alpine, I waited with the bear trap door open. The billy had recovered from the drug and was on his feet in the trap but seemed content to stay inside. He felt secure in the dark culvert after the stressful dog situation he had experienced on the deck. Finally, after a bit of time, the billy's head poked out of the door and he edged his way out, stepping into his new mountain home range. He wandered off as if nothing had happened, not even looking back to thank me.

Although I counted goats from choppers, that was the only live mountain goat I ever had the opportunity to work with or relocate. It was definitely one of my more memorable days as a CO.

7

COASTAL GRIZZLY

I t was July 13, 1987, and we were just heating up the barbeque, waiting for our friends John and Robyn to arrive for a planned supper, when the phone rang at our Hagensborg home. It seemed that was often when a call came in; just when you didn't need it. The caller was a resident up the Bella Coola Valley, near the Nusatsum River, who advised that two grizzlies had shown up in his yard and were acting strangely. During those years, the grizzlies in the lower part of the Bella Coola Valley were usually quite nocturnal, having learned that showing themselves in the daylight around rural homes usually posed a serious health risk to them.

The call seemed a little strange to me based on the time of day, but I dropped supper plans and left Shannon with Robyn once she arrived. Heading up valley, I picked John up along the way. John had worked at the Snootli Creek Hatchery for years and had a great deal of grizzly bear encounter experience. Plus, he knew his away around firearms. The Bella Coola CO posting was a one-person detachment at the time, so getting a knowledgeable bush person to help me was always a huge asset.

Once we arrived at the residence, the complainant advised that the bears appeared to be a sow and a two-year-old cub, almost as big as her. They had been eyeing up and loitering around his corralled pigs, and their mid-day behaviour just seemed strange. In addition, the sow was wearing a radio collar.

Out behind the house, we found the bears bedded at the rear of the yard. I glassed them through binoculars from a safe distance, and sure enough, a radio collar was visible on the reddy-brown coloured sow. The second bear was indeed a cub and was almost as large as she was. The sow was an average-sized female grizzly but looked thin. They were not acting like typical wild grizzlies, which would normally move off when encountering humans. These bears were acting very indifferent to people moving about, which made me suspicious of their origin. Eventually, they rose from their day beds and moved away from the house, disappearing into the thick coastal timber toward the Nusatsum River. One of the bears appeared to be limping, but they moved off quickly, so we had little opportunity to study the bears thoroughly.

I could have dispatched both bears right then and there, as bears that show no fear of humans usually end up in conflict posing serious risks to local residents. With the sow wearing a radio collar though, I thought I'd best check with the area biologists to find out if anyone might know where they came from, or if the bear was part of an important or ongoing study. The only grizzly study that had been ongoing that I was aware of was up at the top end of the Dean Channel, on the Kimsquit River. It made no sense that one of those bears would make its way over the mountains to the Bella Coola Valley with a cub and start eyeing up pigs for a meal.

However, having seen the two-year-old cub limp, I figured I'd best talk to the complainants a bit and ask if they had shot at the bears prior to our arrival. After a short question and answer period, one of the residents finally admitted to shooting a .22 rifle into the ground in front of the bears in an attempt to move them off. He said that perhaps the slug ricocheted off the ground and struck one of the bears. I found this explanation a little convenient and dubious but now needed to confirm if we did, in fact, have a wounded grizzly on our hands.

After numerous phone calls, I couldn't find a biologist who knew anything about the sow. I was still puzzled by the bears' appearance and behaviour in the valley, but head office did give me the okay to destroy a grizzly if it was wounded and not wearing a radio collar.

With the knowledge that the cub may have been shot, I felt I should reassess it if possible. A sow with a wounded two-year-old was nothing for any of the residents (or us) to mess around with. Sow grizzlies have a completely different outlook on the world around them compared to the boars. They can be very aggressive when around their cubs, and with this one potentially having an injured cub, this was very serious business now.

Rolling our eyes at each other knowing what we had to do at this point, John and I loaded our rifles and crept into the dense bush moving very, very slowly, stopping every few feet to look for an ear, patch of hair or slight movement. About 100 yards into the bush, we spotted a small patch of brown fur and through binoculars located the duo bedded under a large cedar tree. I had my trusty 7 mm Remington Magnum with me and was literally "loaded for bear." In full stealth mode, we crept to within fifty metres of the bears, but it was difficult to get a good look at the cub as it was lying on the far side of the sow. After fifteen minutes or so, the pair got up and simply moved off out of sight. The quick glimpse we got of the two-year-old before it disappeared behind the cedar didn't indicate an injury, so we let them move off as it was getting near dusk now. I figured we would continue the saga in the morning light, but little did I know what lay in store for us.

Before going home for the night, we visited all the neighbouring residences to advise of the bears' presence in the area, and that something was off with their behaviour. Although valley folks were used to seeing bears in their yards, I did not want anyone to get into a conflict with these grizzlies.

Later that evening, after I had dropped John off at his home and had finally washed down the last of my cold supper, the phone rang again. One of the neighbours I had spoken with near the bear's last location was on the line and advised that the sow grizzly was going in and out of his chicken coop killing birds. Again, I motored up the valley only to find that the bears had been there fifteen minutes prior and had not returned. As we spoke, we could hear dogs barking feverishly farther down the road, therefore I headed over to the noise, only to find the bears had passed through the yard just moments before. This occurred a couple more times at nearby homes, but the bears were just ahead of me each time. I eventually returned to the chicken coop, parked the truck where I had a good view, and settled in with the homeowner to wait for their return.

Once a bear obtains food, it will always come back for more, it's just a matter of time. We sat waiting for three hours, but the bears failed to show. I thought perhaps the bears had gotten their fill of chicken for now and may not show up again that night. Having to leave the owner on his own, he pulled out his trusty old 12-gauge shotgun loaded with slugs for protection, and we discussed their possible return. I told him that if they returned and started raising hell again, go ahead and kill her if he was presented with a good clean shot. After 11:00 p.m. I fell into bed wondering where the bears had come from, and how this was all going to play out.

At 7:30 am the phone rang: it was the owner of the chickens. He advised the sow had returned shortly after I had left, and he had taken a shot at her. When asked if he had hit her, he didn't have a definite answer for me but felt he had probably killed it. The bear had only reacted by running off after he had shot at her. Although running off after a mortal hit is common for a bear, this was getting bad now. The thought of trying to find a grizzly that may or may not be wounded or dead, with a cub that may or may not be wounded, was more than a little unsettling.

Saying goodbye to Shannon, she told me, "Be careful," to which I gave the standard answer: "Yep, don't worry." Arriving at the site, I surveyed the immediate area for any sign of blood from the bear, but only found a single drop, which could have come from an unfortunate chicken for all I knew. I knew at that point I needed help, so I left to find some.

Again, John and I hooked up, and I also looked up David, a local cougar hunter who owned a few hounds. Knowing that the dogs were actually cougar dogs and not bear dogs bothered me a bit, but I figured the dogs might at least give us an edge and alert us to the bear's presence in the bush. I needed all the edge I could get if I was going to seriously search for the bears now. Both men agreed without hesitation to help. Before we left John's house though, I told him to bring along his .44 Magnum revolver, just in case.

We gathered up our gear and made our way up the valley in David's old International truck, with three hounds in the rear. Once at the site, we let the dogs out of the tall panelled truck box. One hound was a redbone, Major, and the other two were Plott hounds, Mork and Mindy. I was packing my 7 mm Remington Magnum rifle and my .357 Magnum Smith and Wesson service revolver in a high-rise holster. Both John and David were packing .30-06 rifles. John also strapped on his single action .44 Magnum Ruger Blackhawk pistol. The guys knew this was serious business. I told them there would be no messing around with these bears now, and that we were very likely going to get charged if we encountered them. It had unfortunately become a shoot-on-sight scenario, but hopefully, between three dogs, three rifles, two pistols and some bush savvy, we would get the upper hand on the bears.

As we left and headed into the bush, I noted that one of the dogs had emptied his bowels right beside the truck, leaving a t-rex-sized manure pile behind. I jokingly commented to the guys that no doubt someone was going to step in it before the day was over. We all chuckled and carried on.

The dogs were quiet as we made a large circuit in the bush behind the house, but finding no sign of the bears we circled our way back to the house. It had been my experience that wounded animals will move toward water, so this time we struck out toward the Nusatsum River. Not too far into the bush, the dogs began to get somewhat excited and sound off. We knew they were picking up the scent of something and figured it was a good bet that the bears had passed through here. David said he was going to let the dogs off their leash to perhaps flush the bears. I told him that they were likely to get killed if they met the wounded sow in the thick bush. David said that he knew that but chose to let them go anyway. Looking back at it now, that was a bad idea. The three hounds ran off in front of us but immediately stopped barking.

We were now near a large gravel bank on the east side of a side-channel but still well inside the bush. With a shell in the chamber and the safety on so as not to endanger the guys, I led the group with John immediately behind me heading in the basic direction the dogs had gone. We were lined up in single file about eight feet apart now. The wind had come up, so there was a lot of overhead noise in the trees. To add to the noise, we were only forty metres from the rumbling white water of the Nusatsum River. We couldn't hear much, which is never a good thing on a bear complaint … but here we were right in the thick of it. The cedar trees had become spindly and tight, and unlike the more open mature timber we had already passed through, the thigh-deep low underbrush we were now in pulled at our legs.

The dogs had been gone five minutes now, and I was getting a little worried and frankly a bit frustrated at their quiet disappearance. As I turned back to mention this to the guys, John pointed past me, quietly saying he thought he had just heard something ahead of us. At that instant, from fifteen feet away, a brown blur exploded out of the underbrush and headed straight for me.

It was so low to the ground, I thought it was Major returning. Then, as fast as that thought entered my mind, I realized this was no dog. This was a grizzly coming in on a headlong charge. With my rifle at hip level, I pivoted it toward the bear and hollered, "Shoot!" while instinctively pulling hard on the trigger once, then twice … But nothing happened. I was shocked. My trusty old rifle was failing me when I needed it most. The grizzly was closing in at lightning speed, and my rifle would not fire, no matter how hard I pulled the trigger. We were in serious trouble.

From the time I saw her explode out of the bush until she hit me was two or three seconds. It's amazing the things that go through your mind when the shit's hitting the fan. My mind was working incredibly fast, trying to focus on and sort out the details of what was happening. I guess it went into automatic pilot, for lack of a better explanation. I was taught that a person will revert to their training in high-stress situations. That's why training over and over again is crucial for jobs that deal with dangerous situations. My focus was on two things and two things alone: the bear was about to make contact, and my rifle was failing me. I was in deep shit.

To this day I don't know if I fell backward or if she knocked me over. That one second between when my rifle failed to fire and I was on my back is a complete blank. Perhaps my subconscious mind tried to be in a different time and place right then, I don't know. Regardless, I was now on my back, with my arms up for defence, while a very agitated sow grizzly bear was standing on my thigh gnawing on my left forearm like a buzz saw.

I had lost my rifle during the fall, but realistically, it wouldn't have been any use to me anyway with her right on top of me. My focus was on her roaring jaws just inches from my face as she worked my forearm over. At that point in my four-year career, I had only investigated a couple of grizzly bear attacks but knew from what I had read that they always go for the head if exposed. She could chew on my arm all day and I'd be "okay," but I knew that if she got hold of my face or head I'd be in big trouble. I don't think this went on for too long, maybe ten seconds; all the while I was trying to keep her off my head by pushing up on her with my arms. Somewhere in the fray, I hollered, "Shoot!" a second time and the sow let go of my left arm and went for my face. Instinctively, I jammed my right hand into her mouth to push her head back.

John and David were standing only a few feet away, watching in disbelief as the event unfolded in a matter of seconds. They knew they needed to shoot—and fast. They were also frightfully aware they might hit me instead. But when I pushed the grizzly up slightly, John saw his opening and shot her immediately. David, slightly behind and to the side of John fired an instant later. To this day, John says that moment was terrible, and it played like a broken record over and over again in his mind for a long time.

I never heard any rifle shots or felt any reaction from the bear. The next thing my peripheral vision caught was a human leg stepping into view on the left side of my head. I vaguely recall a rifle muzzle coming in and touching the bear on its left shoulder; it was David's. Why the sow didn't drop me at that moment and go for him at point-blank range, I will never know; likely, she was simply focused on eliminating the first perceived threat, which was me.

The sow stiffened up over me, giving me the split second I needed to get my .357 out and shoot at her head. The shot went off, and she rolled off me right away. I was up in an instant and John asked if I was all right, but in my adrenaline rush all I could blurt was: "The bitch almost chewed my arm off!"

John still smiles today when he recalls that moment. But the sow was only doing what came naturally to her. She was protecting her cub, so my heated description of her was totally unfair. I guess I was a little worked up. The sow was still thrashing and roaring on the ground at that point, so I told John to "Shoot her again!" which he did.

We thought for a brief moment that it was all over; then without warning the second bear came blasting out of the underbrush from twenty feet away. It bluff-charged to within six feet before stopping and turning around and running back a bit. It stopped broadside at ten metres huffing and clacking its teeth, obviously confused and agitated. I could see the two-year-old cub wasn't showing any signs of being injured. It had obviously been behind the sow when she charged but had held back from totally committing and following her right in until now. Meanwhile, Major had appeared from out of nowhere and was now jumping all over the sow, sounding off like he should have been doing all along.

I recall as if it was yesterday when John tried to rack another round in the chamber of his .30-06. It was jammed. In his hurry to reload, he had inadvertently short-stroked the bolt and failed to completely eject the empty casing. So when he attempted to close the bolt, a live round jammed behind the empty casing and made the rifle useless until completely cleared. That takes time— which John didn't have. I remember how he calmly leaned the rifle against a tree, drew that long .44 Magnum from its holster, cocked it, and fired a round every time the cub bluff-charged. Meanwhile, David fired with his .30-06, but the two-year-old did not go down. Its adrenaline was also running very high.

I had five shots left in my revolver, and leaning over a log, I also began focusing on my front sight and touched off a shot as well. My rifle had failed, so I wasn't about to pick it up and use it. That fifty-yard pistol shooting at our annual firearms qualification was now paying dividends (in my mind). We all used to joke about how pointless the fifty-yard pistol shooting was, believing we as COs would never use our pistols at that distance. Of course, it was not fifty yards to the bear, but once again, the mind does strange things when it is highly stressed. I was reverting to my old training scenarios.

The two-year-old ran off out of sight toward the river, and as we gathered our wits we heard one of the dogs yelping in that direction. David blurted that one of the dogs was getting eaten, but I said that the dog was on its own. I was leaking blood bad and needed to get out of the bush before I passed out, otherwise, I believed they might be carrying me out. John and David heard the bear slide down the gravel bank and quickly ran out of sight toward the bear, thinking they may have an opportunity to dispatch it. I heard a volley of shots ring out, then all was quiet.

The two-year-old cub had briefly tangled with one of the dogs, then ran out into the side channel and stood there confused. John and David each fired two more shots with their rifles, and the bear finally collapsed into the water. John hollered up to me to ensure I was okay and to stay put, then turned only to see the cub get up once more. Again, they each fired two more shots and the bear again fell and finally drifted downstream out of sight. The tenacity of the two-year-old had been incredible.

Locating my rifle, I picked it up to make it safe and found that the safety was actually still "on." I was in disbelief. My old 7 mm hadn't actually failed me. In the heat of the moment, I had failed to click the safety off when the charge occurred. I learned a hard lesson that day: never go into a grizzly complaint (or any other incident where unexpected crap could happen) with the safety on. Cradling my rifle under my right arm, I supported my left forearm, which appeared to be broken, with my right hand and started making my way to the truck. Stopping to take a brief look at the sow, I could see that she was in terribly malnourished condition and probably weighed 150 pounds less than what her normal healthy weight would have been. She was gaunt, with her backbone vertebrae poking at her hide from beneath for the entire length of her back. I briefly wondered why her condition was so bad, then decided I'd best get out of the bush.

Sow grizzly bear immediately following
encounter with Keith, John and David

The guys weren't far behind me, and we shouted back and forth at each other from a distance as we paralleled each other back to the truck, where we all arrived at the same time. The complainant's wife was out on the porch and asked if we had gotten the bears. One of the guys told her that we had and to call an ambulance, at which time she saw my red, leaking condition and promptly vanished back inside the house. A short time later she reappeared with a clean cloth diaper to help stop the bleeding.

Meanwhile, Major had returned to the truck with David and John after they had pulled the hound away from the sow. However, already sitting *inside* the truck box were Mork and Mindy. The grizzlies had frightened them so badly, they had run back to the truck and scaled the seven-foot racks without us. At that point we had a few choice words for those hounds. Then we loaded ourselves and Major into the truck to leave. I found that I couldn't pull myself into the cab given the condition of my arms and hands, so John pulled me into the passenger side by the back of my belt. David then fired up the old International and we headed out of the yard toward the Bella Coola hospital or the ambulance, whichever came first. Right then John made a squeamish face and said, "Keith, look at your finger." I hadn't noticed, but my right middle finger was badly smashed and pointing back at me over the top of my hand at a very unnatural angle. Luckily it hadn't been my trigger finger.

David put the pedal to the metal, and we headed for town. Partway through Hagensborg though, the engine began making odd noises. Both John and I told David that the engine was going to blow, but David was so determined to get us to the hospital, he never let up on the gas. Soon, the truck slowed to a puttering stall at the roadside. We knew the old International was played out. Right about then we noticed an ambulance casually coming up the highway toward us, so we began waving at them. Everybody pretty much knew everybody in the valley, so the two paramedics pleasantly waved back at us and kept on driving. They must have noticed our frantic expressions though since they slowed a bit when they were almost past. We hopped out of the truck and thankfully managed to flag them down. Apparently they had not received the call.

We relayed the events to the attendants as they quickly placed me into the ambulance, and I told John and David I'd see them at the hospital. By now, the bleeding seemed to have slowed somewhat but they still insisted on laying me on the gurney as they headed for the Bella Coola hospital. Then, part way to town a familiar odour began to emanate inside the ambulance and it struck me. … I'd been the lucky one to step in the humongous pile of dog crap beside the truck. Lovely! My Vibram-soled boots had performed flawlessly on that front. They were loaded. The ambulance attendants were notably not impressed, especially given the long ride back to the hospital. Highways was replacing all the bridges, so we had to keep detouring and slowing down over rough patches of road.

When we finally made it to the hospital, I suppose I was still in a bit of denial that I was actually injured. I was more worried about the serious explaining I would have to do with Shannon. The last thing she had said to me when I headed out that morning was: "Be careful." After I had left home she had gone up to visit John's wife, Robyn, and at the time their place was just across the Nusatsum River from the bear incident, about half a mile away as the crow flies. They'd heard all the shooting, which sounded more like a war going on than a bear complaint, but presumed we had dispatched the bears without any problem. That was until David called and delicately told Shannon, "Yep, we got the bears, but Keith's been chewed on."

Of course, everyone came down to see how I was doing. I was okay but my clothes did not fare so well. The doctor had cut every piece of clothing off me except my underwear, leaving only my boots, revolver and holster intact. When Shannon arrived, that's what she was handed, dog crap and all.

Turned out that my left arm was not actually broken; it just looked like it due to all the swelling caused by the bite damage. A bone in my left wrist had been crushed though, and the middle finger on my right hand was badly crushed and disfigured. My hand had made its way into the sow's mouth when I was trying to keep her off me. They straightened it as much as possible, and of everything the hospital staff did to me, that's what really hurt.

The sow had bitten and punctured my left arm as many times as she could between my elbow and hand and clawed the inner thigh and knee area of my left leg. Shannon said that when the doctor relayed his findings to her, he hadn't been sure what kind of loose parts he was going to find in my pants due to the rips and tears in my pants' crotch area. All three of us were relieved that everything was still intact.

Sometime later, I recall the Chief CO from Victoria calling me to see how I was doing, but with the Demerol in full effect, I really don't remember what I said to him. Shannon eventually removed the phone receiver off my chest where it lay after I had drifted off. After 120 stitches, a finger splint, lots of Demerol, a nasty infection, a gallon of penicillin and a week of hospital time, I was ready to put the event behind me.

I took a month off work to recuperate completely and have to admit that I was fairly jumpy in the bush for a while. During the first week back to work a black bear complaint came in that I attended with a local Mountie. The bear had been killing pigs. Making our way in through the heavily treed area, I put myself in the rear (gee, wasn't that nice of me), as I was still a little jumpy. We crept through the bush on a trail about six-feet wide and focused on the pig's fenced-in area twenty yards ahead. Suddenly we heard a woof behind us, and whipped around to see a large black bear standing up on his hind legs only ten feet from us. It had been bedded behind a large downed tree, and we'd walked right passed it. That was the last mistake that bear ever made. The Mountie then asked, "What is it with you and bears anyway?" My response contained some colourful descriptors.

I went back to the grizzly scene a month or so after being back at work and took Ben, our black lab, with me. As always, Ben liked to run around and sniff things out, so while he did that, I checked out the site. For some reason, it didn't seem the same as I had remembered it. But when I heard an animal running toward me in the bush, my adrenaline immediately shot upward for a few seconds until I realized it was only Ben. I was still a little jumpy at bush noises. I shook my head and figured we'd been in there long enough, so I bailed out of the bush with Ben in tow.

Other than being skittish in the bush for a few months, the event itself never really bothered me too much. It had not surprised me that the sow charged when we got close to her. We'll never know if the dogs encountered and pushed the bears toward us or not, or if we had simply walked into the grizzlies' bedding area. I suspect it was the latter. Either way, the sow charged us as soon as we were inside her comfort zone. Though John and David never so much as told me, I know that having to watch their buddy get rototilled by a grizzly must have haunted them for a long time.

It took quite a while, but I finally pieced all the facts together about the sow and her cub. The carcass of the two-year-old cub had been located downstream a week after the incident, and upon examination, it appeared to have not been injured prior to its death. However, a small .22 calibre entry wound would have been difficult to distinguish alongside the many other gunshot wounds, especially after the bear's body had been exposed in the water for a number of days.

I learned there had originally been two cubs. The family unit had been live-trapped by Terrace COs at the Alcan landfill near Kemano, British Columbia, and relocated farther inland. Grizzlies are notorious for travelling great distances and returning to where they were originally caught, so it's not that surprising they were caught a second time at the landfill. This time they were airlifted and taken even farther inland into the northern part of Tweedsmuir Park. One of the cubs, unfortunately, died from the drugging at that time, but the sow was radio-collared for tracking purposes and released with her lone two-year-old cub.

Once a coastal bear, always a coastal bear, and accordingly the sow headed back toward the coast via the first major river drainage she encountered, the Dean River, which flows southwest toward the central coast. I discovered this in a discussion with a Dean River angling guide, who had spotted a sow grizzly wearing a radio collar accompanied by a single large cub on the Dean River earlier that summer. The Dean River Valley has its own healthy population of grizzlies, as do most coastal inlets, and she likely got pushed from area to area by other grizzly bears, having to defend her cub along the way. Now it was clear why she had been in such poor condition.

From the Dean River, it was only sixty kilometres as the crow flies over the mountains to Bella Coola. Pushed out by other bears, she left the Dean River and entered the Bella Coola Valley, which was the first major drainage she would have encountered to the south. Severely malnourished, she was going to obtain food any way she could, hence the livestock and chickens. This also made it clear why she was behaving the way she was, that is, not nocturnal and with no real fear of humans; she was not a Bella Coola bear. She was a habituated dump bear from the Kitimat area.

Keith and Shannon at Governor General Medal
of Bravery ceremony in Ottawa

A year later I received a letter from Government House in Ottawa. John, David and I were to receive Canada's Medal of Bravery for the incident. We were all very shocked and humbled. A few months later we attended the event at Government House. I was in awe of the ceremony and of meeting Governor General Jeanne Sauve in person, who made the presentations. I got a real charge out of the Governor General's Foot Guards who stood statue-like at the doors and other notable locations. One guard in the presentation room took the time to ask us about our bear encounter and mentioned how his tall black uniform hat was made from black bear hide.

Looking back and having since attended and investigated numerous bear maulings over the years, I can truly appreciate how very fortunate I was with my encounter. Grizzlies will usually bite the head if exposed. I have seen victims whose ears and scalps have been completely or partially torn off, or with entire muscles torn from the bone, causing permanent disfigurement even after plastic surgery. When we encountered the sow that fateful July day, she was making her last stand. She had been trapped, drugged and moved. She had fought off other bears, defended and provided for her cub and tried to obtain food, all the while trying to get home. It was a very sad end for three bears that, enticed by human-produced food and waste, ultimately succumbed to their habituation.

I am forever indebted to John and David for their calm and cool-minded actions. While not all maulings result in death, they likely saved my life that day.

8

THE WINTER
OF '96

Winters affect the different species of wildlife in various ways, and many factors contribute to the wellbeing or demise of animals during those harsh months. The winter of 1996 in the Peace Country was unlike any I had experienced before, and it proved most difficult for the mule deer.

For some genetic reason, mule deer tend to be an easier-going ungulate than whitetail deer. Many of the small towns and rural areas in British Columbia are home to mule deer that have become habituated to gardens, ornamental shrubs, seed crops, alfalfa and stackyards. Along with the attraction to human-produced food sources comes the trait of losing their fear of humans over time, especially during the cold and hungry winter months. It's not uncommon for people to approach very closely to these deer at times, and there have been many cases of mule deer putting the run on people and domestic animals that get too close. Whitetails, on the other hand, tend to be flightier, and rarely allow humans to get close. They normally spook and run when encountering humans, even during winter months. These "domestic" tendencies of mule deer, unfortunately, led them down a cold and deadly path during the winter of 1996.

Mule deer are browsers but also nibble on grasses and succulent plants between spring and fall. This means they have a varied diet of roughage, which their digestive system has become accustomed to over the millennia. Alfalfa, however, is their Achilles' heel, and both mule and whitetail deer cannot resist it. They literally become addicted to it, and mule deer seasonal ranges have actually changed somewhat over the years due to the availability of these agricultural hay crops. During the summer months, the succulent alfalfa leaves provide high levels of carbohydrates, and this is mixed with their other sources of browse which they feed on while living in and around their bedding areas. Therefore, during the summer and fall months, a heavy percentage of alfalfa in their mixed diet is tolerated by their complex digestive system.

By late fall the fawns, having been born in June, have grown substantially, but they still lack the mass and bodyweight of an adult deer. However, fawns still put on large amounts of fat appropriate for their body sizes. Then in late November at the onset of winter, the does (females) go into heat and the rut starts. At this point, the bucks (males) stop nearly all foraging and do nothing but pursue the does for breeding. This also includes being chased off by more dominant bucks when a doe in heat is located, and occasionally locking antlers with another buck over the rights to breed her. By the end of the rut, the bucks have lost the majority of the fat they put on over the easy summer months, just as winter is really starting to set in.

This particular winter the snow was quite deep, and the temperatures were cold, but there had been more than one substantial warm spell, which had created heavy hard crusts in the snow at various depths. For the deer, this made it not only tough for walking and running, it made it impossible for them to paw through the snow to reach any forage on the ground that they would normally have been able to access. There was one occasion that season when I attended an injured deer at the roadside, assuming it had been involved in a vehicle collision. However, the deer had actually jumped a barbed-wire fence and landed in heavy, plowed, frozen snow and snapped both front legs. This no doubt happened on many occasions, and it's likely that most unfortunate victims were not discovered.

As the winter months progressed, more and more mule deer made their way into hay stackyards and simply began to live there. They were hungry and cold, and no longer ventured out to find any typical winter forage. Deer residing in stackyards is common during most Peace winters, in the sense that they spend a lot of time feeding there, but they normally wander off to bed elsewhere or to find browse in bush areas. Not this winter. Now they had become totally dependent on the dry and baled alfalfa, spending all their time in the hay yards. Their "domestic" traits really began to control their movements, and the deer expended as little energy as possible, ate as much as possible and moved very little. They would simply stand and feed, then lie right back down again, or perhaps move fifty feet to where a more dominant deer would not bother or push them away.

There is a very real pecking order associated with mule deer at winter food sources. The mature bucks have feeding rights over all others, with the young bucks and mature does next in line. The young does are next, with the fawns coming last. Each age class will move the lesser class off until they are done feeding. It is not uncommon for a doe deer to strike at her fawns with her front hooves and move them off until she has had her fill. Then the fawns may be allowed to feed next to her, or often they will wait until she moves off. So, there are many different stresses placed on deer in addition to the winter elements. And all these stresses add up.

Large buck mule winterkilled and frozen in round bale feeder

Toward the latter part of winter, the "yarding" of deer in the stackyards really began to take its toll. With bellies full of nothing but alfalfa chaff, their digestive systems began to fail. Their stomach bacteria could no longer process the rich feed. That and the extreme cold weather stressed their systems so badly that they began to get scours (diarrhea). The first deer to succumb to this process were the rutted-out thin bucks, as well as the fawns due to their small body size.

Scours causes a loss of bodily fluids, which in itself is unhealthy, but it also means the body needs to take on more water. The only water available when it's minus thirty degrees Celsius is snow. Although deer and other animals normally eat snow for moisture throughout the winter months, the deer's systems could not handle the excessive amount of snow they were now consuming. They had no ability to fight off the cold that had already invaded their bodies, so the more snow they consumed the more their internal temperatures continued to drop. Then, just like when you or I have a cold, their noses began to run and soon large blocks of ice (or snotsicles, as I called them) began to accumulate on the front of their snouts, blocking their ability to feed.

Now you had mule deer that were not moving, had full stomachs, digestive systems that were not functioning, scours draining their bodily fluids, a lowered body temperature and ice blocking their mouth and nose. There was only one result: death where they lay.

On a cold March day, I drove out to an Upper Cutbank ranch after receiving a call from the owner who reported deer dead and dying in his stackyard. Walking out to the stackyard, dozens of deer stood glassy-eyed, watching me walk past only a few feet away. Many deer appeared to be curled up sleeping at the base of the big round bales. However, the "sleeping" deer were frozen solid. They had lain down for the last time and simply froze to death.

In one round bale feeder, a big mature buck had crawled through the steel bars to bed down in the soft hay, almost as if he was the king of the castle and this feeder was his and his alone. He had lain his head along his side, gone to sleep, and simply never woke up. When we tried to pull him out of the feeder, both antlers popped off his head; it was getting late in the winter, close to the time their antlers would normally fall off. We stood there, each with an antler in hand, staring at each other and then back at the buck. It was very sad.

In another area nearby, the rancher had built a weather break for his cattle out of upright slabs. One of the boards had come loose and fallen off, and the deer could squeeze through the ten-inch vertical opening as a shortcut to the hay. A small doe had gone down onto her stomach as she stepped through the opening and never got back up. She was frozen dead where she had fallen, and her head hung lifelessly over the bottom rail. It was if she had been too exhausted to get back up and, instead, let the lower rail support her head and went to sleep, never to wake up. It was tough to see. I left the ranch that March day with over twenty frozen deer carcasses in the back of my truck and visited other ranches experiencing the same die-off.

Keith's patrol truck filled with winterkilled, frozen mule-deer carcasses upon leaving a Peace Country farm

Prior to 1996 when driving through certain agricultural areas of the Peace, a person could often see one or two hundred mule deer in a morning. After that winter it was never the same, and rather than seeing herds of twenty or thirty deer together, three or four was the common herd size. When fishing on the Peace River the following summer, I found many mule deer buck carcasses in riverside areas where they had wintered, and these were not even in stackyards. I could tell they had died late in winter, as the large pedicles where their antlers had been attached were bare, indicating the antlers had been shed prior to death.

The winter of '96 was a bad one and a sad phenomenon that I, as a lover of wildlife, will not soon forget.

9

BULL-TROUT
TWIST

A fisherman came to me about a guy he knew who had been snowmobiling into Monkman Lake, south of Tumbler Ridge, and catching and keeping large bull trout. Monkman Lake is a beautiful sub-alpine lake in a lovely mountain setting where the bull trout grow very large. But bull trout are suckers for any kind of bait or shiny lures thrown at them and can easily be overfished. As such, they are heavily protected in British Columbia. They can grow to a very large size, often twenty pounds or more, and getting to that size takes many years, many vulnerable years. As a result, the retention of bull trout in Monkman Lake was prohibited. The complainant showed me a photograph he had recently taken on a hike to the lake, depicting a large number of filleted fish carcasses that had been left behind on the shore. His information was credible, as his wife happened to babysit at the suspect's house at times. She had overheard the suspect talking about numerous ten-pound fish he had caught in Monkman Lake that were in his freezer.

I appreciated this tip, as many successes in the law-enforcement world rely on members of the public coming forward with information. Without the public's help, the majority of cases involving illegal resource activities would likely go unsolved.

With the detailed information, I approached the local Justice of the Peace for a residential search warrant, which was approved. Back in those days obtaining a search warrant wasn't nearly as cumbersome as it is today; often a one-page ITO (information to obtain a search warrant) was all that was required to satisfy the Justice of the Peace. Nowadays, ITOs are several pages long as significantly more detail is required. Anyhow, I picked a day with my partner, Shawn, to search the suspect's residence in Dawson Creek. The suspect was at work, but his wife was home. We produced the warrant, so she let us into the house, and we began our search.

We rarely performed search warrants in an aggressive manner, so we asked her if she would mind showing us the house freezer. We already knew we were going to search the freezer and we had the legal right to do it, but in most cases, it helped to calm the situation if a bit of manners was used. In this case, we were dealing with a quasi-criminal fisheries act offence, not a dangerous criminal investigation. It was, however, quite common for people we investigated for resource violations to be involved in criminal activities of some type.

Opening the freezer, we found a basket load of large bull trout looking back at us. We ended the search there but asked if there were any more bull trout in the house. The missus advised there were not. A day later when we finally caught up with the suspect, we charged him with the possession of bull trout and issued him a hefty fine.

As a result of the file information, we began to make more frequent patrols to the Monkman area. Unfortunately, it was not uncommon for vulnerable fisheries to become abused once word of good fishing spread. So, one warm summer day we were parked at the Monkman Lake trailhead monitoring a parked vehicle. From where we were parked in a logging block, it was a two-kilometre trail-hike to the lake. Just the lone pickup truck was parked in the cut block, and with the day getting late we knew it wouldn't take long for the owner to show up unless they had gone in for an overnighter. So, we parked the truck and prepared to sit and wait until dark.

It didn't take more than half an hour before we could see a man walking along the trail through the trees in the distance. Once he entered the cut block and our truck was apparently in his view, he stopped and tossed something off the side of the trail. We walked over and met the fellow as he ambled over to us, and he advised that he had hiked into Monkman Lake alone that day. He said the fishing had been wonderful, and he had released all the trout he had landed.

He denied throwing anything off the trail, but a quick search down the trail behind a log produced a plastic bag containing a fresh eight-pound bull trout. When confronted with the trout, the angler admitted to catching and keeping it. He thought that taking the one fish home wouldn't hurt, because he had apparently hooked it deep in the throat and felt it would die anyway if released. After a discussion of events a violation ticket was issued to the angler, and we all ended our day.

Here is the twist ... that angler was the very same person who had reported the initial bull trout violation just a couple of months earlier.

10

PAYBACK

November 1997 had come and gone, and winter had started to set in. The mule deer were feeling their oats now, and the bucks were in rut and travelling, searching for receptive does in heat. Their necks swollen, they wandered constantly with their heads down, nosing the ground and sniffing other deer tracks for scent left by a doe deer's interdigital gland. During this time bucks' attitudes change. They leave the bachelor groups they have lived in during the summer and early fall months and become more aggressive. Any medium-sized pine tree that happens to stand in their path will likely take a severe thrashing or at least loose a good chunk of its bark and lower branches due to heavy antler rubbing.

Much to the chagrin of rural property owners, bucks are particularly fond of expensive evergreen and ornamental trees, as they are usually just the right size and proportion to bring on an unprovoked attack. Often standing alone in a yard, ornamental trees are eye candy to a buck and are irresistible targets that draw in love-hungry bucks looking to unleash pent-up rutting energy.

A call came in early that December from a landowner west of Dawson Creek, in the Groundbirch area, that a deer was apparently tangled up in their yard. Asking the complainant for more detail, it became clear that an ornamental Scotch pine in their yard had become victimized by a large mule deer buck. In preparation for winter, the caller had protected the beautiful seven-foot pine tree by tightly wrapping it in one-quarter inch poly rope, in the same fashion a Christmas tree is wrapped for purchase. The large buck had apparently chosen that particular tree as his target, thinking he would teach it a lesson in humility, even though the little pine tree's limbs were bound tightly with yellow poly rope. While speaking to me on the phone, the caller was watching the event unfold, describing in vivid detail how the buck was wildly fighting the rope that had become entangled in its antlers. The frantic deer was now firmly tethered to the pine. I advised the caller that I was on my way and would be there as quickly as I could (not really knowing how I was going to deal with the situation).

Arriving shortly after the call, the landowner was excitedly waiting at the front door and quickly explained once again what had happened. He went on to state that the deer had escaped just prior to my arrival. Relieved that I wouldn't have to improvise some method to release the deer, I replied that it was good that the buck had managed to free himself and get away unharmed. Walking out to the side of the house though, it immediately became apparent that the buck had not completely freed itself, but had escaped with the little pine still attached and in tow. Though I felt bad for the property owner's loss, I had to choke back a chuckle when I envisioned what had likely transpired with the buck.

The Scotch pine had no doubt been expensive to purchase and had been nurtured along to about Christmas tree size for a few years. Yet now, only a ragged, sad-looking, splintered stump, about three inches in diameter and six inches long stood as a reminder in the middle of the frozen yard. The snowy area around the stump had been completely trampled, looking like a small war had taken place in a twenty-foot radius. The landowner also couldn't help but chuckle when he described how the buck had fought the rope that held him firmly by the antlers, and how it had made countless thrashing circles around the tree until the trunk finally twisted and broke off. The buck had then run off in terror with the tree trailing behind it. Being held to the deer's antlers by a length of rope that put the tree right at the buck's rump, the little pine had slashed and whipped the buck's rump and haunches as it had headed for the next quarter section as fast as its four legs could carry it. As such, it would seem that the little pine had given some payback to the buck and gotten the last laugh.

Grinning, I followed the bounding tracks through the shallow snow across the property, while potential scenes played out in my mind. I envisioned the terrified buck tearing across the yard at warp speed, with a Christmas tree slapping its butt at each and every bound. A hundred yards out, I could see the buck had encountered a barbed-wire fence while on a flat-out-forty-kilometre-an-hour run. It had easily cleared the fence, but the little pine inflicted another blow and ended its journey there. At a slower speed, this would have only flipped the buck around, stopping it, and entangled it in the fence for a second tug of war. But the deer must have been travelling so hard and fast that the rope snapped tight and broke as the buck's momentum hurled it forward. A clear splash in the snow was present where the deer had done an end-over-end and hit the ground when the slack had come out of the rope. The buck had then regained its footing and bolted wildly off across the field, finally freed of the rump-whipping pine hoodlum.

There, lying on the ground at the fence with a short length of yellow poly rope attached was the saddest version of a Charlie Brown Christmas tree I had ever seen. Not a needle or limb remained, and only a stubby, barkless beat-down remnant of what once was a full, perfectly shaped pine tree now lay in the snow. It was a sad sight, but that pine had managed to get the last laugh on that buck deer. The little tree had laid a good licking on the buck's hind end as payback for all the other pine trees the buck had no doubt raked and ravaged with its antlers over the years.

I never did see the buck, but the evidence showed it left the area on a dead run with a good length of rope still tangled in its antlers. It is probably still running today, and probably never stops to bully any pine trees along the way!

11

TALEOMEY CRIB TOURNAMENT

The central coast area of British Columbia is a wild and beautiful place. The deep, dark inlet waters lined with steep, rugged peaks are intriguing and tend to draw people back, especially if they're fond of the wilderness and wildlife. My years spent working in the Bella Coola area hold many great memories, and some still make me chuckle when I recall them. It seems adventures involving bears and bear complaints always bring back vivid memories. One such adventure always comes to mind when I sit down for a game of crib.

A logging camp at the bottom end of South Bentinck Arm had called in a bear complaint. A bear had broken into a camp home, scaring the occupants badly. Being that the complaint was in a remote fly or boat-in area of the district, getting a wheeled culvert trap to the site was not possible. So, I gathered up my snare equipment, my trusty rifle, a few clothes and sleeping bag and headed to the Hagensborg airstrip.

Arrangements had been made for the logging company to pick me up in their private aircraft, which turned out to be a twin-engine Navajo. I was riding in style to this complaint, enjoying the twenty-minute flight, until I noticed oil leaking from the right wing. Fortunately, nothing transpired from that issue. We flew west along the Bella Coola Valley and out over North Bentinck Arm. From there the little twin-engine aircraft banked south and headed down South Bentinck Arm to the Taleomey Valley, located near its southernmost tip. The plane turned east up the long Taleomey River, which is home to many black and grizzly bears, and within a few minutes touched down at a remote airstrip near the logging camp.

At the landing strip, a man driving a white crew-cab Ford F250 4x4 met me and introduced himself as John. Meanwhile, the Navajo powered its way down the gravel strip, quickly lifted off and disappeared from view down the mountainous inlet. We piled into the truck along with my gear, and John drove us back to the camp. As we bounced along the rocky logging road, John started to tell me about the large black bear that was hanging around the area, and how it had actually broken into their house. John was a man in his late fifties, who seemed a little crusty around the edges. He really didn't like small talk very much, and got straight to the point describing the bear incident to me the very moment I got in and slammed the truck door shut. I noticed right away that John wore very thick glasses and leaned forward in an exaggerated manner over the steering wheel. He also seemed to squint at the road while he drove. It made me wonder if he perhaps had some serious vision problems. Since he was driving, that worried me a little bit.

Driving through the camp area, I began to notice how quiet things were. John explained to me that he and his wife were presently the only ones in the camp, all alone doing the caretaking. No wonder the black bear was so bold. The camp was quiet, and the bear had undisturbed, free roaming access throughout the camp and buildings. Soon we pulled up to a decent double-wide mobile home that was actually very nice for a camp setting. Sometimes living quarters in remote camps such as this were pretty rough, but John's home seemed very tidy for a remote logging camp. I pulled out my gear and headed to the house, while John continued his non-stop details about the bear without letting me get settled in first.

Inviting me in, John introduced me to his wife, Anne, who greeted me. She seemed very pleasant and hospitable, but it was immediately apparent that she was blind. Right then I realized the severity of this particular bear problem. Having a bear breaking into a home occupied by people with vision problems was serious business indeed.

Settling in and storing my gear in one of the rooms, I went into the kitchen where a coffee greeted me, and John began once again to relive the bear occurrences. They had seen the bear around the entire camp area, but one evening at dusk when returning to the house after doing camp chores, they found the front door broken in. Cautiously John had entered, finding the kitchen in shambles. Dog kibbles had been scattered about, and items were lying on the floor. His obvious concern was that the bear was actually still inside. Luckily, John found that the bear had left out the back through the screen door. As Anne was quite vulnerable, both were very anxious that the bear might return in the night. John explained that Anne had been blind since childhood, and that although he could see well enough to function and carry out day-to-day chores, his own vision had deteriorated enough over the years to the point where optometrists had deemed him technically blind. He went on to explain though, that the camp-caretaking-business suited them well, and that they really enjoyed it.

John showed me his high-tech home-defence system, a 12-gauge Winchester Defender shotgun, and then explained how the bear had actually returned after dark. He had nearly opened fire on the bear through the screen door, but with his poor vision and the low light, he could only see a black blob on the porch, so he held off. I told him that he was wise to have held off shooting given the circumstances. He could have created even greater problems if he had wounded it. Plus, he would have wrecked the screen door. John agreed but insisted he re-enact how he had seen it through the door.

I admit in no uncertain terms, I was extremely dubious about John's shooting abilities with the Defender and discussed the general use of the shotgun with him. He insisted that he was proficient with it, stating that he would have to show me how he shot with it. Changing the subject back to the bear, I began to ask specific questions about its behaviour, and if there was anywhere, in particular, they had seen it more than once. John advised that they had seen it coming out of the bush a few times, at the far end of the clearing from where the house was situated. Bears are notorious creatures of habit, especially if they have obtained food previously, so I asked John to show me the spot.

It was the perfect location for an ambush site. It was a bit of a pinch point clearing with numerous large trees at its edge where I could fashion a cubby and attach a leg-hold snare. My plan was to set the snare then stay in the area if need be for a few days until it was caught and I could dispatch it, or until it showed itself in the camp area and offered me a free-ranging rifle shot. Though destroying any animal was not a pleasant part of my work, live-trapping, tranquillizing and successfully relocating a habituated raiding camp bear had little chance of success. In addition, the remote setting did not allow for any relocation equipment, and helicopters were not normally used to relocate black bears. Therefore, the decision to dispatch the unfortunate bruin had been predetermined before leaving home. Plus, the bear had broken my unwritten rule of physically breaking into a home.

The snare was placed at the base of a stout fir tree twelve inches in diameter, and I took the time to make a good job of it as I wanted to be sure of catching this bear if it provided the chance. (I described how a bear snare functions in chapter two).

Although I was somewhat confident that we were dealing with a black bear due to the daylight sightings by John, grizzly bears roamed throughout the area as well. Catching one of the often-nocturnal grizzly bears by accident was a real possibility and a consideration for safety. Upon finishing the set-up, two tall sticks were placed against the tree so that if the snare cubby was disturbed, they would topple and alert me from a distance that perhaps something had indeed been captured. The sticks were visible from the kitchen window with binoculars. Satisfied that the snare set-up was as good as it was going to get, I needed bait. I asked John if he had any bait, and he said they had a freezer full of meat. This was going to be easy it seemed. I then asked him if he had a tiger torch so the meat could be burned a bit, making it aromatic and easy for a bear to smell and locate.

We headed to the house freezer, but along the way, John advised that he knew where there was some unthawed pork. Into the kitchen he went and came back out with a beautiful pork roast that Anne had taken out for supper. I told John that frozen meat would most definitely do, but he brushed it off saying that Anne could make something else for supper. I tried to talk him out of it, but John insisted in his normal crusty growl, so I reluctantly complied. We nicely browned the roast with the tiger torch and it smelled wonderful. I chuckled to myself about using Anne's supper for bear bait, but knew it would be too tempting for the bear to pass up if it came through the area. I felt bad for John's wife and cringed thinking about the conversation that was bound to occur between her and John once she discovered supper had been kidnapped.

The day had progressed into the late afternoon by the time the snare equipment was set up, so John took the opportunity to bring out the Defender and demonstrate his shooting abilities. Empty pop cans were lined up against a dirt pile, and he proceeded to load the shotgun for some serious buckshot and slug action. Ensuring that I remained safely behind him, I fully expected John to start his first volley of shots by using a firm two-handed grip on the stubby Defender. This particular Defender had no shoulder stock

73

and only possessed a rear pistol grip. Maintaining a solid two-handed grip when the firearm was recoiling from the heavy slug loads would be difficult, as there was no rear stock to help absorb the recoil.

John raised the shotgun to take his first shot, and to my utter shock, he held it out at arm's length like a pistol with one hand and let 'er rip. Needless to say, it bucked into a vertical position, like a green packhorse whose rear cinch had slipped into areas where it shouldn't be. When the dust cleared, there wasn't so much as a blemish on any cans. Three shots later we began to have a discussion about his stance and how he held the shotgun. John was adamant that this was the best and most accurate method by which to unload the weapon on all targets, then touched off another two rounds. When it was all over and dirt, rocks and dust had settled, there were definitely pop cans lying everywhere, but I was certain the carnage was only the result of rocks and debris flying everywhere. I was relieved that John had not opened up on the bear the night it had come back to his door. Who knows what condition his living room and kitchen would have been in by the time the shotgun was empty, let alone the bear.

With the shooting session safely behind us, we went back into the house where I am sure the married couple had a very lively discussion about the pork roast. I kept myself busy digging out my sleeping bag and organizing my gear. As it turned out, John's wife put together a wonderful steak dinner on short notice. Then after supper before it got dark, I checked the snare and camp area, but there was no sign of the bear.

As the evening progressed a crib board surfaced, and my hosts indicated they would like to have a game. I was amazed that two visually impaired people would, or even could, consider playing crib, but I gladly accepted the invitation. Right away I noticed that the cards had Braille markings on them, and Anne pulled out a Chinese abacus for scoring. She informed us that she would keep score for all three of us, and I was astounded. This was going to be different, but I really looked forward to how this was going to transpire.

As we started playing our cards in turn to thirty-one, it became clear that when a ten-point face card was played, John and I had to state if it was king or queen, etc., as Anne could not "pair" the card without knowing what actual face card was. She was extremely adept at playing her cards using the Braille markings and had absolutely no problem counting her hands accurately at the end of each round.

In contrast, John could not read Braille, yet his eyesight was so poor that he had to hold his cards three inches from his nose to read them. He would consistently miss points in his hand. After a few times where I noted he had missed some points, I thought I would help him by letting him know that he had missed the points. Well, that was a serious mistake on my part, and John told me in no uncertain terms to mind my own cotton pickin' business, and that he would count his own damn crib points. Well okay then, it didn't take me long to learn that lesson. So I kept my mouth shut on that front for the rest of the evening, and was entertained by John's card counting (or lack thereof) all night. As John and I would count our own hands, so would Anne, then with quick adeptness, she would move the beads on the abacus, and tally everyone's points. It was an entertaining evening that I will never forget. Anne and I took turns at winning crib games, while John's cribbage abilities were right along the same lines as his shooting abilities.

At first light, I was up and keen to see if the offending bear was caught in my snare, but through the binoculars the two undisturbed sticks were still leaning casually against the base of the tree, indicating nothing had been disturbed. Disappointed that the bear had not returned, I settled in for my morning coffee while Anne whipped up a nice breakfast. It was a clear day on the coast, and I envisioned doing some exploring around the area and enjoying the scenery. But as soon as breakfast was done, I headed up to the snare to have a closer inspection.

I meandered up through the 100-yard clearing from the house toward the snare. At fifty yards I suddenly noticed that the leaning sticks, which had been undisturbed only half an hour earlier, were now down! Holy ol' hell, something had happened during breakfast! Stopping and watching the snare intently, all appeared quiet. Nothing moved. No bear. Now I was getting upset with myself, as I figured the bear had come in while I was lazily sitting sipping coffee and eating bacon, stole the bait and left.

Cursing under my breath, I approached the snare. Then, at twenty feet, a very large and agitated black bear, marked with a white chevron on its chest, stood up and huffed aggressively at me while clacking its teeth. Frankly, I was shocked that a bear was caught, as it had been very quiet upon my approach. Additionally, I had let my guard down in that last forty yards, and that bothered me.

It was over in a second, and the offending bruin would not bother the camp or its occupants anymore. It was a large adult boar that weighed about 300 pounds and had only been caught and held by one front toe. It was quite possible that had I not checked the snare it may have pulled out of it fairly quickly. Both John and Anne were relieved that they no longer had to worry about the big black bear breaking into their home during the night, and I was satisfied that I had helped them out by solving their problem.

We needed to dispose of the bear carcass away from the camp area, and John quickly volunteered to transport it out toward the coast with his pickup. Thinking about my own safety, I asked if he would like me to drive, but he insisted in his crusty manner that he would drive. So away we went, down the valley in the old white Ford with John leaning over the steering wheel so he could see the gravel road. As we got farther down the valley, the road made its way from the river bottom up onto the steep mountain sidehill, which dropped a long way down to South Bentinck Arm below. The road wound its way along the mountainside, with a vertical cliff on the upper side, and a sheer drop-off on the lower side. I was certain I was doomed to end my days careening over the cliff edge with crusty John madly cranking at the steering wheel. I don't know how we made it, but finally, a ravine appeared that would suffice for disposing of the bear, and the truck rattled to a stop. There was barely enough room to turn a Smart car around on the narrow logging road, let alone a long box crew-cab pickup. But after John's twenty-five-point turn and putting the rear bumper over the cliff edge just as many times, we had the Ford headed in the opposite direction and made it safely back to the camp.

Later that day, I was picked up by the Navajo plane once again and headed back to civilization. I was relieved when the leaky plane finally touched down on the Hagensborg strip safely and I could make my way home. It had been an interesting two days, including a crib tournament that I wouldn't soon forget.

12

START
LOOKING UP

It was summertime and a call came in from a rural family who lived right behind our office near the Hagensborg airport. They had let their small family dog out for a run and were mortified when a cougar quickly appeared and grabbed it. The little pooch was the perfect size for a tasty cougar morsel. Luckily the family ran outside hollering, which managed to scare the cougar off their dog. The dog was quite badly scratched and bitten but survived the sudden attack.

I called the local hounds-man who came over right away, and we began following the scent trail. His hounds usually did a good job of picking up the scent and following the trail, but on several occasions after treeing a cougar the hounds would seem to lose interest and stop baying. They would just loiter in the vicinity of the tree only occasionally sounding off with a random trademark bark or howl. As a result, I got into the habit of looking up and searching the treetops in the area whenever the dogs stopped baying and began wandering aimlessly.

The scent trail led from the house through the mature coastal cedar forest to our office building, around the chain-link fence surrounding the warehouse, across the road and into the bush heading east up the valley. As the scent trail seemed hot and fresh the hounds were keen to go. We let them go and heard them feverishly baying as they followed the cat's trail, in typical cougar-hound fashion.

The baying grew quieter as the dogs pulled away from us, but eventually, after twenty minutes of sweaty bushwhacking, we began to close in on the dogs. As we neared the dog's location, I realized they were not as excited about the whole affair as they should be. They had stopped baying in their typical excited hound-dog fashion, and were wandering aimlessly among the trees.

I immediately became suspicious, and about that time the lead hound, Major, walked back toward me, stopped at the base of the big cedar I was standing under, and let out one lame "Arrooooof!" My spidey senses kicked in, and I slowly looked upward into the cedar's branches. Glaring down at me from no more than eight feet was a mature male cougar perched on a thick limb. That was the last dog that cougar ever attempted to eat for supper, and the last time I ever got caught not looking up when I should have been.

13

SISTER MARY

I feel a tad sheepish relaying this tale, yet I really was in a bind and backed into a corner by the events that took place. Heading to the Squamish area was a day trip for many folks living in the Lower Mainland, so it was popular with many who liked to fish. There are a few lakes that lie right alongside Highway 99 that are home to small trout, and I would often find people angling on foot for the rainbows and cutthroats that lived in these lakes.

One summer day while heading home from a Whistler bear complaint, my partner, Paul, and I spotted three people angling along the shoreline of Brohm Lake. Pulling in, we quickly realized the anglers were nuns.

Mom was Catholic and raised us that way, and as such I attended a private Catholic school during my grade school years. Most of my teachers during those early years were nuns, and I remember them all as being the nicest teachers I ever had. I remember how they wore the traditional long black-and-white dress, or habit, and a flowing black-and-white headdress. As the years went by, the habits became knee-length dresses, and their headgear became skimpier, allowing more of their hair to be seen.

I could not recall ever having run into an angling nun before, but there was a first time for everything, so I ambled over and struck up a pleasant conversation. We discussed the niceties of angling, the weather and every other subject I could bring to mind but knew at some point I would have to ask about licences. I felt a twinge of guilt for even thinking about it, but after a little while, I managed to summon enough courage to ask them if they had happened to pick up fishing licences at some point before venturing out for the day. I was surprised when they responded right away that no, they did not have fishing licences. The brief thought of even possibly writing them up for angling without a licence horrified me. Therefore, without hesitation, I chose to simply advise them that the next time they went fishing to be sure to pick up licences first. They said they would and thanked me, and Paul and I went on our way. Of course, all the way home Paul ribbed me for being too "soft" and not even writing a warning. I advised Paul to take it easy on me and explained how I had gone to a Catholic school as a kid and had been an altar boy during that time. Jokingly, I told him that if I ticketed a nun I'd go to hell for darn sure.

Later that summer, to my astonishment we spotted a black-and-white habit along the shoreline of Brohm Lake for a second time. I hesitated in even stopping and thought about totally avoiding the awkward scenario, but our work conscience (and curiosity) got the better of us. I cranked the steering wheel and pulled in to park. This time the angler was alone, just Sister Mary by herself. Once again, we had a stress-free conversation until I had to broach the subject of the number of lines she was angling with. She was using spinning gear, and unless using fly fishing gear from a boat, lone anglers were restricted to one line. I politely explained the regulation to her, and she promptly reeled in the extra line.

Now the angling licence issue came up. Not again! No licence had been bought, and she had also bonked a few small rainbows to take back to the convent this time. She explained she hadn't gotten around to buying a licence yet. Well, this was twice now, so being very polite I figured I'd best make it a little more formal, so I wrote her a check-up slip. The check-up slip was normally used to require an angler who did not have their licence with them to produce it at a later date. In this case though, it was used as a warning. I took no issue with the fish she had kept and simply ignored them, knowing I would be taking the check down a difficult, awkward slope if I did so. I also knew she was making good use of the fish.

I felt a little guilty writing the warning, but it was the second time in as many months, and most other anglers without a licence would simply have received a ticket at that point. I got the feeling that Sister Mary kind of knew what she was doing. I justified it to myself, hoping the warning might give me a get-out-of-hell-free card, and left Sister Mary on good terms. When I got back in the truck, I really got the gears from Paul though. I had to struggle hard to defend my honour.

The following May, Paul and I were heading south on Highway 99, and when passing Murrin Lake saw a number of people angling from the shoreline trail. We pulled in, and to save time we split up and walked in opposite directions around the lake. I took the highway side, Paul the bush side. The trail along the highway side was wide and in the open, and about 100 yards ahead of me on the trail was a person partially concealed by a large boulder. I could make out a bit of black clothing but did not think too much of it. Then I noticed two rods propped up and their lines extended out into the lake on the far side of the rock, set line style (a weighted lure is cast out, sinks to the bottom, the slackline is reeled up, and the rod is propped up and watched for a nibble). About that time, the person's head poked out from behind the rock and looked my way. I recognized Sister Mary right away. Oh boy, here we go again with the two line issue! Immediately she vanished behind the boulder, and I could see one of the rod tips vigorously shaking from being reeled in.

I am not a religious man, but right then I looked up and said, "This is a test, right?!" Not wanting to make a scene, I hot-stepped my way to the boulder, and there was Sister Mary madly reeling in one of the two rods with a strange look on her face. Once again, I struck up a pleasant conversation and advised her that she shouldn't be fishing with two rods. Right away she said she knew it was wrong, but she just keeps doing it. Now I started to get the feeling that she had been playing me all along with her niceties. This time I did not hesitate in asking if she had bought a fishing licence yet. The answer was no. I couldn't believe the position Sister Mary had put me in. I politely advised her to reel in and come along with me to the parking lot.

Sister Mary left for home with a ticket that day. Paul, well, he never let me live it down. And me, well, I'm going to hell … I know it.

14

RIGHT PLACE, RIGHT TIME

Catching and keeping too many fish can be equated to many other types of "guilty mind" offences. That is, when people know what they are doing (and do whatever it takes to get away with the deed). During my service in Bella Coola, I often got vague reports of people over-limiting on salmon while staying at unknown residences or large camps. They would bring freezers into the valley and store fish where there was power, which made finding and checking those freezers difficult. An angler might be checked by myself or fisheries officers while on the river, but the total number of fish that person may have kept elsewhere was unknown. If they had illegal fish stashed, they would leave the valley with the fish when they knew the coast was most likely clear. Once as far as Williams Lake and out on Highway 97, the chances of being checked for fish were remote.

Alexis Creek CO Ken and I were coming back across the long, dark and vacant Chilcotin Highway very late one night. We had made a midnight run to Alexis Creek to quarter and hang an illegal moose carcass that we had seized at dusk. It was mid-October, and the moose rut was just starting to wind down, but the coho fishing in the Bella Coola Valley was still going strong. Coho salmon run up the Bella Coola and Atnarko Rivers from the North Bentinck Arm between August and October and the fall event was extremely popular with resident and non-resident anglers. Tired from a long day of checking hunters and non-stop driving, we were looking forward to bunking in at a cabin we had rented at Nimpo Lake and enjoying a well-deserved shot of whiskey before hitting the hay.

At three o'clock in the morning, around a distant corner just east of Tatla Lake, headlights appeared. As we neared, it was apparent the vehicle was a pickup truck stopped in the middle of the road. We stopped, fully intending to simply help someone with perhaps a vehicle problem. I approached the driver and introduced myself to three middle-aged men. The driver said they were having light problems. When asked if they had been doing any hunting or fishing, he said they had been hunting, but there was no hunting gear inside the cab (albeit, it was the middle of the night, but there should have been a cased rifle or some other hunting gear visible). As Ken came up to the passenger window and started a conversation with the far guy, I went to the rear of the truck and looked in the box, where there was a freezer. When asked what was in the freezer, the driver said they had some fish belonging to a friend, however, he couldn't come up with the friend's name. Pulling the freezer out onto the tailgate, I opened it and found it loaded with frozen coho salmon in the ten to fifteen-pound range. I counted twenty-one: nine over their combined possession limit of four fish each. That totaled around 250 pounds of salmon, and I recognized the "greed factor" associated with these guys. Again, the driver said some belonged to a friend but when asked for the name again, he mumbled an unrecognizable response.

It turned out the three men were brothers from the Cariboo. I held their attention at the truck while Ken wrote them fines. When we served them their paperwork, I advised the fish were being seized, and Ken backed our truck up to theirs and began loading the freezer. One of the passengers stated we might have the right to seize the fish, but the freezer was private property. He was informed in no uncertain terms that the freezer was also seized, but might be returned upon conclusion of the case. Then one of them asked what the saltwater possession limit on coho salmon was (assuming it was more than four per person) and began to concoct a story about catching the fish on the ocean. I said the saltwater possession limit was eight fish each, but we knew better and quickly dispelled that BS theory.

At that point, they began to become more agitated and belligerent, and the driver blurted, "If this makes it into the papers, I'll have your balls!" Not wanting to get into a verbal battle with the trio, we finished the seizure and service of documents and started to leave. The driver finished the conversation with, "You guys are sure lucky to get us this time," then added a final, "F--- off!" as we parted company.

We were more than a little ecstatic that we had encountered the brothers, who were obviously old hands at the illegal salmon game and had probably gotten away with it many times before. We had ourselves a dandy drink of whiskey at five o'clock in the morning to celebrate a great day of busting bad guys in the Chilcotin. However, I think I grew a little greyer around the edges that night, thinking and wondering about how many resource abusers like this trio may have slipped by me over the years.

15

THE PLAN

As I explained earlier, the winter of 1996 in the Peace Country was a particularly bad one for ungulates due to the deep snow and cold temperatures. Mule deer had suffered a terrible die off, and moose were also impacted. Moose are browsers, normally eating twigs and branches, unlike grazers such as elk. So typically, snow depth does not affect moose much. However, the snow that winter was deep and crusty enough that many ended up wintering at farms and ranches for the easy access to hay in the stackyards. Many moose managed to eke out a living through the hard winter months of 1996, only to succumb to heavy infestations of winter ticks on them in April.

Moose have obvious personalities: some are easy going and some tend to be a little more aggressive. Put a somewhat aggressive moose into a hungry, stressful winter scenario, and it could get very possessive about its food source. I received a complaint of an aggressive cow moose loitering around a farmyard. The cow would not let a young couple get any hay from the barn for their horses. Getting caught on foot by a moose can result in some serious injuries, so something needed to be done.

Pulling into the yard, I immediately spotted the cow moose loitering at the barn before I even talked to the complainants. The landowner met me at the door and acknowledged the moose by the barn was indeed the culprit. As a first attempt, I figured I would try to move it off somehow. Often, pushing a moose off did not work for very long; they would often return. But, putting a serious spook into a moose was occasionally enough motivation for it to move off for good. It was worth a try.

Not wanting to put the moose down unless left with no other option, I pondered a plan. This particular rural property was very open and quite flat, with only a few stands of leafless winter poplar here and there. The closest heavy cover was a stand of pine off in the distance a few hundred yards away. I had no cracker shells with me for noise making, only my rifle. Normally I didn't use noise much anyway, as most times a loud noise really didn't affect a moose. They usually needed to be hit with something thrown at them to really get their attention and spook them, such as a block of wood or a rubber bullet. I could try running at her, but with a foot of snow on the ground, that would be chancy with an aggressive moose. When dealing with an agitated moose, I always liked to be near a barn, truck or some other type of cover that I could duck into or behind quickly. Running after a moose on foot across an open snowy field would not be wise unless I was prepared to wear white coveralls and dive into the snow if it turned to charge me, and well, that was not going to happen.

I got back into the truck and pulled it closer to the barn where she was standing. I wanted to see how she would react. Right away she moved off a bit into the open away from the barn. Suddenly the plan materialized: It dawned on me that I was sitting in a large, loud, fast piece of moose-hazing equipment beside a nice flat open field. Without a second thought, I turned on the siren, hit the gas, put the pedal to the metal and headed straight at the cow across the field.

That long-legged gangly cow moose lit out of there like her tail was on fire, with me going flat out not twenty feet off her rear bumper. Well now, this plan was taking perfect shape according to me, and across the field we went with her at a dead run. I was a little unsure how the 4x4 would make it through the deep snow, but it was powdery enough and I had a big enough head of steam that it plowed across the field no problem. I had no intention whatsoever of letting up on the gas until I pushed her to the distant timber. She needed to know that she was not welcome at this farm, and I was just the guy to teach her that lesson.

About a quarter-mile out we were both clipping along at thirty kilometres an hour, and with a grin, I was getting great satisfaction out of thinking my well-devised plan was coming together in perfect form. Suddenly the cow's rear feet went out from under her. She did the splits and went into a headlong snowplow. To my utter shock, it hit me that in my haste to prove my point, I had unknowingly pushed her right across the flat, snowy field onto a snow-covered pond. I really should have been concerned about the well-being of the cow moose at that point, but in all honesty, all that entered my mind was the paperwork involved in explaining this to the boss, if they had to winch my truck out of ten feet of frozen water with a drowned cow moose pinned beneath. It would not be good.

Fortunately, the cow regained her footing, got up and carried on at a dead run, and my truck was still on the top side of the ice, which was good. However, self-preservation was setting in. Although it was common to see ice fishermen's vehicles on lakes during winter months, many private ponds had aerators that caused the ice to remain thin during winter. So without hesitation, I held my breath, kept my speed up, and eased the steering wheel over to make a gentle turn back to where I thought the shoreline should be. Of course, it was late winter, and the ice was probably two feet thick, but my little brain could only think of the worst-case scenario.

Breathing a sigh of relief, I finally made it back to shore without incident and brought the pickup to a stop once I knew the truck was back on terra firma. Looking back to see how the moose had faired, I was relieved to see her still high stepping it into the distant stand of pine, apparently no worse for wear. The plan had worked, sort of, as she never did return that winter.

16

GARFIELD

They say laughter is the best medicine. Shannon and I have played a lot of practical jokes on each other over the years and have had many laughs with each other as a result. We just like to poke each other in the funny bone as much as we can. Although this next cougar complaint was not a practical joke, I still have a lot of laughs about it at Shannon's expense. It involved a cougar on the Saloompt Road on the north side of the Bella Coola River not far from where we lived.

On a fairly average warm summer day, I received a frantic call from a lady who had been riding her bike home on the Saloompt Road. She claimed to have encountered a cougar lying on the front lawn of a home right beside the road. She described how she had seen the cougar outstretched on the lawn, hit her bike's brakes, quickly turned around, and peddled like a person possessed until she got to the safety of a house from where she called me. The caller was Shannon, and she stated in no uncertain terms that she would not ride her bike past the cougar to get home, insisting I pick her up and give her a safe ride home in the truck.

At that time the cougar population in the valley was high, and Shannon was aware of all the cougar complaints I had been recently dealing with. She felt I should know about this one right amongst the rural homes. She had been riding her bike home from a friend's house on the south side of the valley, crossed to the north side of the river via the Bailey Bridge and headed home. About a half-mile farther down the road was where she had encountered the cougar lying in a front yard, just a stone's throw from the pavement.

Snared male cougar. Photo by Keith

Throughout our time together, Shannon has been exposed to pretty much every kind of critter, in various forms of living and non-living condition. She can handle being around the cute, small or lifeless critters, but has a curious aversion to close encounters with live moose, bears and oddly enough even cougars. I suppose it might be understandable, as they can have rather nasty attitudes in close quarters. I told her that she would likely have had no issues if she just peddled on past, but then again, cougars are attracted to fast-moving prey. There was a resounding: "I'm not going anywhere near there on my bike!" on the other end of the phone. Resigning myself to the fact that I would be banished to the dog house if I did not pick her up, I headed over.

Putting her bike in the back of the truck, we drove toward where she had spotted the cougar. Along the way, I listened to a highly animated recounting of events as Shannon described the cougar in detail. She described it as being no less than fifteen feet in length, weighing 600 pounds, and having canine teeth at least six inches long. Based on her description, it must have been the last surviving sabre-toothed tiger. Of course, I had to rub in the fact that she had done an about-face and vacated the area, rather than staying to watch the cat from a distance to see where it might have gone. I ribbed her that she was not a very good wildlife investigator. Seriously though, Shannon did have good reason to be nervous about what had happened; I just failed (accidentally on purpose) to tell her that at the time.

I knew whose yard the cougar had been lying in by the description, and as we neared the home I slowed down and began to look the area over. Seeing no cougar in plain view, we pulled up to the front yard. There, lying on the lawn was a big cat all right: a big orange domestic tabby cat. I roared with laughter and blurted to Shannon: "There's your cougar. It's Garfield!" Shannon was not impressed, stating in no uncertain terms that the tabby cat was NOT the cougar she had seen.

"Does that cat have a tail that's three feet long?" she said. Well, I didn't have a good come-back for that one. She went on to describe the cougar again, including the long tail while I continued laughing, really starting to rub it in now.

I made a thorough search of the area and we spent a lot of time giving each other the gears, but did not see the cougar. Shortly after, I got the local hounds-man to bring his dogs over in an attempt to pick up a scent trail. The dogs indicated a cougar had been present but were unable to sort out the scent trail on that dry summer day. More scent is left behind and is easier for the dogs to pick up when there is moisture on the ground.

Shannon has seen enough cougars over the years to know exactly what they look like, so I have no doubt she did encounter a cougar that day. But I occasionally bring up the topic of Garfield, just to keep things interesting.

Keith on the first day of work as a CO on Monte Lake
with mule deer attacked and chased onto ice by dogs.
Deer was slid to the far side of the lake and released

Brycen and orphaned fawn deer at home in Squamish

Keith checking caribou hunters via helicopter in
Ilgatchuz Mountains near Anahim Lake

Shannon with small black bear cub
relocated to Vancouver Game farm

Conservation Officers in attendance at the 2005
North American Wildlife Enforcement Officers'
Association convention in Penticton, BC

Two mule deer bucks killed by one hunter and subsequently seized
by Keith near Dawson Creek. Smaller buck was left discarded in the
field after larger buck was spotted, shot and taken home by hunter

Keith with a tranquillized young grizzly bear in the
outer coast area of BC. Culvert bear trap in the photo
was custom built for helicopter transport

Snared grizzly bear and equipment being slung out by helicopter

Keith, after being dropped off by helicopter, drifting
the Dean River by raft to check steelhead anglers

School children in attendance at one of Keith's many bear classes

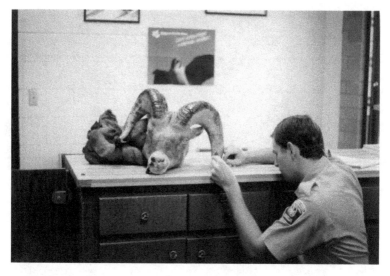

Keith completing a compulsory inspection on a ram head before
the days when horn jigs were provided to district offices

The benefits of CO postings were many, including great fishing.
Keith with 25-pound chinook salmon on Bella Coola River

Trio of black bears tranquillized and readied for relocation
from rehabilitation facility near Dawson Creek

17

PURE SKILL

Having a sixth sense when checking for hunter or angler compliance was always helpful. One clear spring day in the early 1990s, I was up the Squamish River Valley with Brenda, the local fisheries officer. We were checking for anglers and bear hunters up toward the Elaho River. Around the corner came a Blazer, so I threw on the red and blues and pulled the rig over.

I don't remember why, but I took the lead on the check and walked up to the driver's door while Brenda stood close by watching for anything that might catch her attention. The lone male driver was very cordial, and we chatted about what he had done and where he had gone that day. When I commented that he must have been angling earlier in the day due to the fishing rod leaning up over the back seat, he advised that he had, in fact, been angling farther up the valley. When asked how he had made out fishing, he said he had not caught anything.

The daily limits for rainbow trout and dolly varden were quite restrictive in the creeks and rivers in the Lower Mainland. Gear restrictions and bait bans were also in place in the rivers and creeks, so I asked to inspect the gear he had been using, and he quite happily opened the back of the Blazer and handed me his rod. There was nothing outwardly unlawful about the hook and wool tied on his line, but a bare hook and wool are indicative of a roe set-up (fish eggs). Fishing with roe was not legal in the rivers and streams, but of course, the man was not presently angling, therefore I just had to deal with what we had at hand.

Putting the hook to my nose I got a whiff of fish slime, which was probably nothing more than leftover odour from the roe, but I ran with a hunch right then. I asked him why his lure smelled like fish if he had not actually caught any fish, and immediately he admitted to actually catching a few fish. Not wanting to give him any time to make up a story that perhaps he had released them all, I simply asked him where the fish were. With no time to think, he simply stated they were hidden under some gear where the rod had been.

Not only had he killed a creel full of dolly varden, but he was also over-limit by four fish and had killed a number that were undersize (minimum size from a creek or river was 30 cm). Once a fine was issued and the fish were seized, we climbed back in our pickup and continued our day. Brenda, being the investigator she was, began quizzing me about how I knew the guy actually had fish in his truck. She asked, "Was the fish smell on the hook routine just bunch of bull, or what?"

I chuckled and retorted with a cheesy grin, "It was no bull, just pure skill!"

18

HOUDINI
TIMES THREE

I t had been a long Peace Country winter, and spring was a welcome relief to the seemingly endless, cold thirty-below nights. The trees were leafing out now, and visibility into the bush was being reduced as each day passed. The bears were also out in full force now and could be found in most areas where any green groceries were exposed along roadways or in open areas.

An early June call came in that a bear was being a serious nuisance at a rural home west of Dawson Creek, out in the Arras area. The caller quite anxiously described that a black bear was breaking her windows, determined to enter her home. The complainant was an alarmed woman who was alone in her home at the time. I was in the area, so I quickly headed out to what sounded like a fairly serious bear complaint.

Complaints of black bears physically breaking into homes was a rarity. Typically, complaints about black bears were about them making repeated visits to a property to steal dog food, get into garbage containers, or just loiter around. Over the years though, I had generated a pre-determined rule-of-thumb attitude test for bears when deciding if a bear was to be relocated, or alternatively (and unfortunately) destroyed due to safety and habituation concerns. When a bear failed the attitude test and broke into, or attempted to break into a home, it normally bought itself a one-way ticket to the Pearly Gates.

Pulling into the front yard, the complainant was waiting for me, motioning to me from just inside the glass-framed door on the front porch. No bear was in sight, but immediately I could see that panes of glass on the door were broken and lying on the porch. She opened the door a few inches and anxiously greeted me from half inside the door frame. Getting right to the point, she advised that the bear had been there just moments before and had been breaking the windowpanes on the door. I reassured her that I would have a thorough look near the house and around the property right away. I walked back to the truck to retrieve my rifle, knowing what I had to do if the culprit showed itself.

Walking around to the rear of the house, I found myself face to face with an average-sized lone black bear lying on its belly with its head buried in a large bag of dog kibbles. Without hesitation, I dispatched the bear and felt the usual emotions that accompanied the deed, returned my rifle to the truck, and advised the complainant that all was safe now. With hesitation, she peered out the back door to see the culprit now lying on the lawn. I advised her it would no longer be breaking into her home.

Pulling the truck around to the back of the house, I pulled out my ramp and began loading the bear for removal. Upon rolling it over, it was immediately apparent that it was a lactating female. Oh no, this bear had cubs, and the cub or cubs were nearby somewhere. There had been no way of knowing she had a cub. Now I felt awful, knowing that a family unit was involved and that a cub was orphaned. I quickly realized that this complaint was far from being over, and that was an understatement.

Letting the complainant know what I had found, she indicated she had never seen a cub with the bear, so it had never been an issue. I told her I would have to find the cub and try to catch it if possible. So leaving the house, I studied the surrounding tree line at the edge of the back yard for a likely hiding spot. Seeing nothing obvious, I entered the bush and started looking up for the cub. It is common for small cubs of the year to take refuge in trees, while their mother remains on the ground.

Walking into the bush the pleasant sound of spring songbirds filled the forest. The forest floor was quite open, with a mixture of spruce and pine and a few large cottonwoods thrown into the mix. Getting a view up into the heavy evergreens was difficult due to the thick branches, but the three-foot-round cottonwoods were clear to the top with their scaly brick-like bark. Before long, I spotted a fuzzy round black leaf among a clump of branches right at the top of a huge hundred-footer. Throwing up the binoculars I could see it was an ear. Changing the angle from the ground, I could see two ears, then four, then six ... six ears! Six ears meant three cubs, and they were right at the top of the tallest and biggest cottonwood in the area. Their mother had undoubtedly placed them in the best and safest hiding place available near the house. Unfortunately, wildlife's most dangerous enemy, man, was about to make that hiding place not so safe anymore.

They were young cubs of the year, and were cute as buttons, like any new bear cub. The black little fur balls peered down with intense curiosity as I pondered how in the dickens a person might be able to get them down ... alive. They were too small in body size to tranquillize safely without seriously injuring or killing them, and aside from that, they were simply too far up the tree to access. Having tranquillized dozens of bears, big and small over the years, I'd learned that *most* bears could withstand a serious fall to the ground from tremendous heights, reviving themselves seemingly unharmed.

The memory of a little black bear cub I had darted high in a fir tree in Whistler many years before came to mind. It was approaching dark at the time and having run out of options, I elected to attempt a darting shot on the small cub whose mother had been killed by a vehicle. The bead sight on the tranquillizing gun loomed awfully large against the tiny cub's silhouette, but as it settled on the even tinier hind end, I touched off the shot and watched the dart fly true. I was using a smaller, less potent dart to prevent overdosing or killing the little cub. The dart struck, and the utter shock of being hit by the metal dart startled the cub enough that it lost its grip on the branch it was perched on. I was actually quite surprised at the shot accuracy. For a second I was exceedingly proud of the shot I had just made, and that I was about to actually rescue the little guy. That thought came to a crashing halt when the cub fell headlong onto a rock at the base of the tree, and sadly died instantly.

With the memory of that little cub in Whistler still clear in my mind, attempting darting shots at these three tiny cubs was a non-starter for me on this day. Come heck or high water, they would be brought down safely by some other means.

Around this time, the complainant's husband came home, and we pondered the situation. There was no way we could safely get to the top of the tree, so the only real option was to bring the top of the tree down to us. A chainsaw and a few helping hands would likely complete the chore. His neighbour, he said, was a logger and might be able to help us get them down. I gladly accepted his offer and began to make plans on how to capture the cubs if we could get them down. Off he went to ask his friend for help and soon returned with the neighbour and two other friends eager to assist.

His neighbour brought along a length of heavy cotton rope in which he quickly tied a knot on the end, then shimmied up a spruce tree beside the cottonwood. Once up about twenty feet, he shot the rope out and around the cottonwood, just like a lariat being thrown around the back legs of a steer. A slip knot cinched the rope tight around the cottonwood, and he dropped back to the ground. I was amazed at his skill. He made the job look easy.

Once we had a chainsaw in hand and the guys had found two clean garbage cans for make-shift kennels, the plan of how to physically catch the bears was discussed. Bear cubs, even little ones, can run really fast, so I made it clear to them that their window of opportunity to get their hands on the cubs would be very small once the tree came to rest. They would not be able to hesitate, as the cubs would have only one thing on their mind: to get back up the nearest tree as fast as possible. Having said that, I hoped the little guys would not be injured during the tree's fall to the ground. The cubs were settled in among a heavy jumble of leafy cottonwood branches. Hopefully, those branches would help buffer the fall. Once again, my options were limited, so we hoped for the best.

We stretched out the cotton rope at an angle providing the clearest falling lane, keeping in mind that we had to safely stay clear of the tree and falling debris ourselves yet stay close enough to be able to close the distance on three fast-moving cubs. While three of us pulled the rope to control the fall direction, the sound of spring songbirds was drowned out by the chainsaw roaring to life.

The cubs peeked down as the saw made quick work of the front undercut. Then, as the back cut was finished, we pulled the tree to convince it to fall toward the ground in our direction. The big cottonwood began its heavy free fall, and as I lost sight of the bears, we all sprinted a few yards to the side to allow it to fall clear of us. The cottonwood came down hard with brittle limbs breaking off and flying everywhere. The saw was shut off, and it was suddenly quiet and still again, with only the odd branch still falling from the forest canopy above. Immediately, we all ran back toward the treetop to intercept any escaping cubs. The stillness lagged, and I feared the worst for the cubs, but suddenly a black fur ball came streaking out from the jumble of limbs right in front of me. Tunnel vision set in, and I was locked on and running full out through the forest in hot pursuit. It was a thirty-yard dash, and I was not gaining ground. As the cub reached a large pine tree and jumped on to it to start climbing, I made up ground and caught it going up the tree trunk at head level with one hand. The squalling and balling began as I pulled the little guy off the tree by the scruff of the neck, but thankfully the cub was safe and apparently unharmed.

Walking back to the fallen tree, two of the helpers also returned carrying squalling bear cubs in their hands. I hadn't witnessed it, but they too had won foot races and caught cubs. All three cubs seemed healthy and unharmed by the fall. Having chased many bear cubs over the years, successfully catching all three cubs in one attempt was remarkable. But we had done it, and we happily placed the little bears into the makeshift kennels.

The cubs were about the size of house cats but had the temperament of bobcats. They would eagerly nip at any hand that tried to pick them up, but some leather gloves solved that problem.

Thank yous and handshakes to everyone concluded the episode. Then after we wiped the blood off our faces from being scratched and speared by dry branches during our foot races, I left and made my way to see Leona at the local wildlife rehabilitation centre who I hoped could house the cubs. I felt bad about having destroyed the cubs' mother but had rescued her cubs from slow starvation, and there was at least some gratification in that. If I had relocated the group, the habituated sow would have eventually shown up at another rural property and caused similar problems. Chances are the results would have been the same.

At the rehabilitation centre, Leona and I examined the cubs, two females and a male, and all were confirmed healthy and uninjured. They were placed in a large caged enclosure, previously used for holding eagles and fawn deer. I was unsure at the time when the cubs would be released but was relieved that they were safe for now. I knew Leona would take good care of them throughout their stay.

Spring turned to summer, and summer to fall, and the cubs were getting big. The decision had been made to release the bears come fall, and let nature take its course. Cubs released without a mother had a 50/50 chance of survival. Not knowing exactly how to care or den for themselves is challenging for cubs. Over the years, however, I had seen orphaned cubs successfully survive winter, especially if they could find a food source such as a moose carcass. Leona and I on previous occasions had discussed building a den out of straw bales inside one of her enclosures but had not done so to date. We did eventually try this idea and over the years successfully overwintered a number of bear cubs in homemade dens this way, including one grizzly bear cub.

Keeping cubs over the winter means they can be released the following year when they are much bigger and more likely to survive. However, their increased size makes them physically harder to handle. Also, the longer they are in the enclosures the more habituated they become to humans and domestic food. It's a double-edged sword. In this case, the decision was made to release the bears come fall.

As the fall colours began changing the landscape from green to yellow, I received a somewhat frantic call at home one evening from Leona. The bears had escaped from their enclosure. It was almost dark, so the capture would unfortunately have to wait until morning. It was unlikely they would go far, as they did not know the area and were still cubs. I advised Leona I would come over first thing in the morning and find them.

With a quick coffee and breakfast out of the way, I headed straight to the rehab centre and saw where the cubs had chewed and dug their way out of the caged enclosure. Leona and I chatted briefly about the break-out, then I walked to a treed area out behind the enclosure and found the escapees within five minutes. As I approached, they scrambled up a nearby tree. All three were present and accounted for, peering down at me with an innocent "What?" expression on their faces. They had now increased to medium dog size over the summer, so I knew I would have my hands full catching and handling them.

Keith and orphaned black bear cub after a foot race

I headed back to the truck for the catchpole, then back to the base of the tree to wait, but after an hour they had still not come down. Normally a bear will come out of a tree fairly quickly once the threat leaves, but they were out-waiting me, so I left the area to let them come down in peace. Thirty minutes later I crept back into the area and could see the bears were no longer in the tree, but I could hear them breathing down at the tree base. On my hands and knees, I slowly crawled closer and peeked over a downed log. Lying in front of me were all three bears, sound asleep, one with all fours in the air. I choked back a laugh and wished I had a video camera with me at that point.

Unfortunately, I was all alone with only a catchpole to deal with the bears. As I slipped the noose over the head of the nearest cub, it woke with a start and rolled over in an attempt to head for cover, but he was caught. The remaining two blasted back up the tree trunk and stopped to watch while their brother was removed kicking and squalling back to a different enclosure.

All the commotion had made his sisters extremely wary about coming back down the tree, and even after leaving them alone and quiet for an hour, they refused to come down. I had no choice. The tree needed to come down in order to capture the cubs once again.

Returning to the tree with my chainsaw and work partner, I stared up at the cubs and remembered the day they rode the big cottonwood to the ground. With any luck, this catch would go just as well. However, handling both the chainsaw and bear duties would be difficult. Then after a quick review of the ground area, tree number two was heading to the ground. The tree was very top-heavy, and all the branches made it difficult to get to the cubs quickly. As we fought our way into the inner branches, the cubs went out through holes at boot level, and easily headed to a neighbouring tree before we could get clear of the heavy branches clawing at our clothes and faces.

One cub headed up the tree, but the second ran as hard as she could along the ground until she was out of sight in the underbrush. I was in disbelief that we had totally failed on both counts and looked all afternoon for the missing sister, but she was nowhere to be found. All we could do was hope she would show up at a neighbouring property, and that someone would give us a call. As it turned out, we never saw or heard about that cub again. She probably did not survive, unfortunately.

For the remaining cub, it was now highly unlikely she would feel confident enough to come down the tree, even if left alone. Therefore, permission was obtained to cut the third tree down. Once again, a ground plan was discussed with Leona, the chainsaw roared to life and tree number three was coming down with a bear perched in its upper limbs. We had to wonder if the missing sister had actually learned from her two earthward journeys that safety in a tree was no longer a sure thing.

As the tree began to fall, I made certain that I was in a position this time to intercept the running bear, and when it came past I made no mistake. Grabbing the cub by the scruff of the neck was not quite the same this time, as the housecat-sized cub had grown into a twenty-five-pound handful of serious attitude. However, with a heavy two-handed grip soon the sister cub was safely back inside the enclosure with her brother, and the formal release of the remaining two cubs was discussed with Leona in order to bring this bear story to an end.

Releasing the cubs near Leona's home was not an option, as the area was full of rural farms and homes. The cubs would undoubtedly become nuisances in the area and would likely not survive dog or people encounters. However, the culvert trap normally used to catch and relocate bears was at our warehouse in town, and Leona and I both wanted to release these bears before they decided to dig their way out of the enclosure again. Therefore, Leona offered me the immediate use of her sheep crate to move the bears. The crate was eight feet by four feet by four feet, constructed of 2x4s with a vertical sliding door on one end. The door had three-inch gaps, but the gaps on the roof were slightly wider, leading me to suspect the cubs might be able to slip out through the top. I hoped, though, that once the journey got underway, the bears would settle down on the floor and not attempt to climb around. Best-laid plans …

We slid the sheep crate into the rear of my truck box, but it was quite heavy due to being wet. The sliding door was also binding as the wood was wet and swollen from the rain. Oh well, I thought, better than driving all the way to town for the bear trap.

After a brief rodeo in the enclosure with the catchpole, both bear cubs sat sheepishly inside the crate, probably wondering where their sister had gotten to. Not wanting to give the bears any time to explore a way out of their temporary home, I thanked Leona and headed the truck out of the driveway onto the Old Hart Highway to finally put an end to this bear saga. Since I was going past our home, I called Shannon to see if the kids wanted to accompany me on the release, which they eagerly agreed to.

I was settled in for the twenty-minute drive home to pick up the kids and was cruising along the gravel highway when I heard scratching on the roof of the truck. For a second or two it didn't register what the noise was, then suddenly the thought of a bear cub squeezing out the top of the crate and getting onto the roof of the truck struck me. At that moment, a black bear cub slid down off the roof over the passenger side window rear feet first. It slid over the window desperately clawing to stop its descent, until its front claws caught the rain gutter. Hanging there stretched out over the passenger window, it peered helplessly around while my mouth hung open in shock. I couldn't believe what I was seeing.

About the time it sunk in what was happening, the cub dropped off the window and out of sight. Travelling at eighty kilometres an hour, I immediately thought the worst. Hitting the brakes, the truck came to a long sliding stop on the gravel. Jamming the gear shift into reverse, I backed up and could see the gravel spray where the cub had hit the road, but there was no bear in sight.

The break-out had taken place on the country road adjacent to a grassy pasture, and there 100 yards in the distance was my bear cub running hell-bent for election across the field toward the one and only tree … a bushy willow. Once again, I was amazed at how tough and resilient bears could be. It seemed that this particular bear complaint was indeed some kind of a test for me, destined not to end.

Climbing over the barbed wire fence I crossed the field and stood on my tiptoes at the willow, while the escape artist stared down at me. Stretching as far as possible, I was not quite able to reach the cub's head with the catchpole noose without some additional height. Fortunately it was a stunted willow, or it would have been another chainsaw predicament. I needed something to stand on and looking around there was nothing but wide-open field.

During all my field years I carried a five-gallon jerry can of gas in the work truck in case I ran short or came across someone in need of fuel. I used it on a number of occasions over the years, but this day would bring the most important use that jerry can had ever seen. It was now a much needed ladder. The extra height that jerry can provided was just barely enough for me to slip the noose over the cub's head. Out of the willow he came, and we danced all the way across the field, under the fence, and over to the truck.

Being that the crate door was swollen and difficult to slide open, I needed to use both hands. That's when the cub chose to head under the truck. He climbed up under the box and clung on behind the spare tire. Obviously scared, the cub seemed content to cling to the bottom of the truck, so while holding the catchpole between my knees, I tried to raise the crate door, but to no avail. The door was stuck shut, and I did not want to let go of that catchpole. It seemed I was in a bind and needed help.

With the cub glued to the truck undercarriage, I had no choice but to flag down a passing car. The good Samaritans stopped, which was surprising as I was not in uniform. It was a middle-aged woman and her mother. I explained my predicament, advising that they were in no danger from the cubs and that all I required was for them to raise the sliding door for me. It was my lucky day, and unbelievably the woman agreed to help and climbed up onto the crate.

While her mom stood by and took photos, the kind woman stood on the crate and prepared to pull the gate open, but as hard as I tried, I could not pull the cub out from under the truck. The cub was holding onto the undercarriage for dear life. To force the cub out from under the truck, the catchpole noose had to be tightened a bit, and the lack of oxygen caused the bear to slightly relax its grip on the truck. As I pulled the cub from under the truck, the woman pulled on the sliding door, but also to no avail. It was stuck too tight for her as well. With the catchpole secured between my knees again, I helped her raise the door enough to finally fit the cub through.

Lifting the cub up and through the door opening, the woman immediately slammed the door back down with a lot of exuberance and pinned the catchpole against the floor of the crate. Meanwhile, the cub was gasping in an attempt to get more air. We hurriedly raised the door, and I finally released the noose, allowing the cub to regain its air and composure. All the while, the second cub sat watching the entire episode from the back corner.

This whole escapade just would not end for me, and I did not want the little Houdini artists escaping through the roof again. Therefore, I strapped my plywood Ski-Doo ramp on top with ratchet straps to keep the little beggars in. I thanked the good ladies who had stopped to help a complete stranger, then continued on my way. They probably still tell that story today.

A quick stop at the house to pick up Brycen and Nicole, and we were finally on our way to the release point. After many dusty and bumpy miles into the bush, we stopped at a hospitable location where there was water, cover and lots of natural groceries. We opened the gate and after a bit of hesitation, the two cubs sprinted to the nearest pine tree and climbed up. We talked about the bear's chance of survival for a few minutes as they peered down at us curiously. Mixed emotions once again came over me, as only two of the original four family members had survived and these little guys were being left all alone. I shook the thoughts off, knowing full well I had done the best I could throughout the entire saga given the circumstances. Then we closed up the crate, headed home, and finally ended this long, long bear story.

As we rounded the first bend of the rough bush road, Brycen looked over and said, "Geeze, Dad, that sure was easy, eh?" I just gritted my teeth and grinned as the dust rolled up behind the truck.

19

EASY PEASY

ases involving deer, moose and elk being killed out of season were common during my time as a CO. I solved many cases over the years, with a number resulting in very heavy fines, and even some jail time. But just as many cases never got solved because trees and birds can't talk, and often there was simply no evidence to connect the offence to anyone. There is one case that always stands out in my mind though. Not because it was a difficult file to solve, or that huge fines or confiscations were involved, but just because of the way the events transpired.

It was December, the moose seasons were long over, and I received a call from a concerned citizen about a possible moose shot out of season. The information was limited, and all I received was the suspect's name and that he had supposedly shot a moose, that was it. I had no kill location, no carcass, no bullets or shell casings, no actual witnesses, nothing. Just the name and that he may have shot a moose. Certainly not enough information to obtain a search warrant. I had nothing of good evidentiary value to base a case on.

I had no proof of any kind that a kill had even occurred, but I did find out where the man lived and decided to pay him a visit. Though it did not work all the time, there had been a number of occasions when I had absolutely no physical evidence of a misdeed, so I resorted to using my one opening line that often broke the case. Therefore, with the lack of any real evidence, I thought I'd give it a try if there was no other sign of a moose kill at the suspect's home.

Just south of Pouce Coupe, I pulled up to the rural home, which was down a long driveway set back in the timber on a quarter section of land. Looking the property over as I drove through and exited the truck, nothing seemed to indicate a moose had been off-loaded from a vehicle or dragged across the yard. A continual survey as I slowly walked up to the front door also revealed no obvious blood or hair. I hesitated to knock on the door, hoping to spot something that would give away the existence of the deed. Seeing nothing, I finally knocked on the front door and a pleasant middle-aged man appeared. In full uniform, I introduced myself, and about that time his ten-year-old son appeared beside him in the doorway. I said hello to both and then confirmed the man was the person I was looking for. Once that was sorted out, the man wanted to know how he could help me.

Well, there was no point in beating around the bush, so I simply popped my magic opening line in a non-accusatory matter-of-fact tone, "I'm here to talk to you about the moose you shot."

"Moose? What moose? I never shot a moose."

At which point his son curiously looked up at him and blurted, "What do you mean, Dad? What about the two hanging in the garage?"

The man's shoulders sagged, he shook his head in disgust, and he spilled the beans right there. That was all that was involved in solving the entire case, other than seizing *two* moose, a cow and calf hanging in his garage, taking a formal statement, and issuing him a court appearance. Probably the quickest and easiest "closed season" file I ever dealt with.

Just like that … easy peasy.

20

GREY HAIR

s COs, we all undoubtedly had offences get past us without knowing it. I often thought about it, and I suppose ignorance was bliss to a certain extent. Had I known everything that got past me, the grey hair would likely have come in a whole lot sooner than it did. This story involves a young couple on Red Lake near Kamloops in 1984, and watching *another* CO have "one get past him" was a little entertaining, to say the least.

Red Lake is situated north of Savona, lying on the plateau directly north of Kamloops Lake. It is known for its good brook trout fishing. The Kamloops COs were planning some plainclothes patrols to various winter fishing lakes in the area and Red Lake was on the list, so I tagged along to help.

On this particular February day, the plan was to have two of us move around on the target lake for a couple of hours, blend in, do some fishing, and watch for the numbers of fish being caught and by whom. Then Heinz, another Kamloops CO, would patrol the lake on foot. Upon checking us, we would then give Heinz our information on the various anglers and fish numbers. We had our portable radios and would be available by radio whenever Heinz showed up on the lake. It sounded like a workable plan. We drove up to the lake in separate trucks, got our notebooks and ice fishing gear together, and walked out on the lake for the morning's work.

Bob and I headed down the lake on the pleasant mid-winter day and settled in for some "fishing" near what appeared to be the only group on the lake. The group consisted of a young man and woman, along with an older gentleman. Strolling over to them, we asked how the fishing had been, and they said they had already caught a few nice ones which we could plainly see lying on the ice. Asking if they minded if we fished nearby, they said sure and we drilled a couple of holes and did our thing.

The allowable limit was eight fish per person, so the group of three was allowed twenty-four fish if they all managed to catch their limit. Fishing was actually very good, and we had to keep releasing brookies back down the holes in order not to "limit out" and not have a good reason to loiter. The group of three was catching a lot of fish, and soon they started counting their pan-sized fish lying out on the ice, which was good, as they were approaching their limit. Before long they were at the magic number of twenty-four but continued to angle. We figured we might have some folks who Heinz would eventually have to speak with.

After they had caught an additional three fish, the young fellow started talking about how they should leave pretty soon, as they were over their limit. We watched as he started looking nervously around the lake. They chatted about what would happen if they were checked by a game warden, while Bob and I, straining to hear their conversation, chuckled to ourselves. As they talked about the problem, they continued to fish. Soon we could see the figure of a person way down the lake in the distance walking toward us from the parking lot. Although you couldn't make out who it was, we figured it was Heinz, but he was still too far away to see his uniform. The trio eventually saw the unknown person coming down the lake as well and took that as their queue to quit fishing. Had the group continued to retain more fish leading to a gross over limit, Bob and I would have stopped the offence from continuing right then. However, with only three extra fish involved, we thought we would see how this little performance all panned out.

We watched the show as they counted out their twenty-four fish and put them into their ice sled. Then, the young fellow emptied hot chocolate remnants from their large wide-mouth thermos and poked the additional three fish into it. Packing up their remaining gear, they said goodbye and headed off down the lake. Bob and I were actually pretty impressed with their plan, although it was only three fish. Once they were on their way down the lake, we radioed Heinz to alert him about the group and their hidden fish but got no response. We tried continuously until we saw the group encounter Heinz down the lake. There they all stopped, and we could see him checking and talking to them for a few minutes. We knew darn well Heinz would never check the thermos, why would he. Soon the three anglers left Heinz and were on their way down the lake to the parking lot. We continued trying to raise him on the radio, but to no avail.

Ten minutes later Heinz walked up to us in his normal jovial manner. Immediately we asked him what the deal was with his radio, and he got a strange look on his face. Pulling out his radio, he realized he'd forgotten to turn it on. Well, that was pretty darn handy. We asked him how many fish the group had, and he said they had their limit of twenty-four fish. We broke the news to him about the thermos, and he squealed in disgust as we relayed the story to him. Bob and I laughed all the way back to the truck, and Heinz's moaning and squealing continued all the way down the lake. Of course, the group was long gone by the time we got to the parking lot. I bet they also laughed and kept their thermos in a cool, safe place all the way home!

Ah yes, the ones that got past me definitely added to my grey hair, and I think Heinz probably grew a little greyer that day too!

21

PEOPLE

In the bush, you expect to encounter people who have a true interest in doing things closely related to the outdoor environment and what it has to offer. Whether it be fishing, hiking, camping, exploring, photography or whatever, there is something for everyone. It's been my experience that folks in urban areas tend to experience the outdoors less on a daily basis, but eventually head to the rural areas to get away from it all and do their thing, whatever that might be. Mixed in with these folks are people who head to the bush to do, well, "different" things. Or at least things that I found to be a tad curious or different anyway.

Without a doubt, during my years posted in Squamish, I encountered more of these "different" activities than anywhere else in the province. The coastal areas adjacent to the urban Lower Mainland are heavily forested and hold a lot of spectacular mountainous terrain. This, in turn, holds an abundance of hidey-holes for folks to "do their thing," without typically being bothered or perhaps even detected. On weekends, people would leave their city routines and head for the lakes and forests up the Sea-to-Sky Highway, and into the Squamish, Whistler and Pemberton areas where an unsuspecting game warden might happen across them.

Satanic Cults

Sounds a little different right? Well, they are and they exist. A patrol down beyond Lillooet Lake one day put my partner, Paul, and me right in the middle of a satanic camp which was fortunately vacant at the time.

Doing our job in the bush, we were naturally curious about any road or trail we were not familiar with, and always took time to explore them. That was the case on this particular day when we were checking for anglers along a windy road that extended down the northeast side of the Lillooet River. It was always a really long day when we patrolled that area, which made it difficult to get to know all of the out-of-the-way hangouts. I always tried to explore different areas and roads as much as I could though.

Having spotted a little trail that deked off the main road, we naturally turned into it thinking it might lead to a campsite or some hot fishing spot. It led to a campsite all right. Through a long winding goat trail, we entered a camp clearing, but something just seemed off. A large fire pit was surrounded by rows of log benches set in a cross pattern if viewed from above. We did not realize the cross formation at first glance, so we just began poking around a bit, looking for signs of previous activity like we normally would do. It always felt good to get out of the truck and have a stretch and walk around while exploring a camp location.

We came across what looked like a little cairn about two feet tall, constructed of rock and concrete. At first, we thought perhaps it was just a crude version of a fish smoker that someone had built, as it had an opening at the base that had obviously held a small fire at one time. On closer examination though, we noted a piece of cloth lying in the ashes, so we poked at it a bit with a stick. Much to our dismay, we pulled out what appeared to be the remains of women's panties. We both wondered what in the heck we had stumbled upon. A crime scene perhaps? This was getting weird, and my spidey bush senses started to tingle.

We began taking a *very* close look around in case there were any other signs of foul play but found nothing else out of the ordinary except the cross formation of the benches around the fire pit. We were definitely looking over our shoulders by the time we left the area. I recall the hair on the back of my neck was standing straight up as we drove out. We reported our findings to the Pemberton RCMP and soon learned that there had been previous reports of satanic cult activities taking place in that area. We learned that these cults had taken to sacrificing an article of woman's clothing in lieu of a live body in modern times.

Satanic cults, devil-worshipping, human sacrifice—at the end of the day we realized that we had to keep an eye out for people associated with these types of activities. But in terms of their ritualistic beliefs: "Yeah, whatever" was our thought. Of course, we talked a bit about what we had discovered and learned, but other than it being a strange find left it at that.

Sometime later, I heard third hand that a local person had experienced a strange event in the same area. Late one night, near where we had discovered the camp, this person had stopped to offer assistance to a vehicle that was pulled over. He rolled down his window and asked if they needed any help and was absolutely adamant the driver had glowing, red eyes.

As I said, all sorts of folks can be encountered in the bush.

War Reenactors

Without a doubt, I am a history buff. Dad trained to be a fighter pilot during WWII in a Harvard trainer, but fortunately for him, the war ended just as he was preparing to go overseas. Dad's brother did, however, serve overseas during WWII and often showed his battle scar to his kids. I guess my cousins finally came to the realization one day that his scar was located right where his appendix had been removed a number of years previously. I suppose it made for a great story to my cousins, and I'm sure my uncle thoroughly enjoyed pulling the wool over their eyes. All kidding aside, I think I've watched almost every documentary and movie ever made about WWII. I often think about the men and women who witnessed horrible and life-altering events in the wars over the years, and it humbles me to think that most of us today have no inkling of what they must have seen and lived through.

The Squamish CO boundary extended as far north as the height of land between Pemberton and Goldbridge, and we would occasionally drift over the top and check out resource users in Lillooet's area, or even meet up with the COs from the Lillooet office for a patrol. I recall, on one of these patrols, coming across a group of middle-aged men in the Goldbridge area completely decked out in camouflage. This was back in the days when camo clothing was just starting to catch on, and folks wearing it always attracted our attention. One guy in the group said they were re-enacting a war scene.

It also soon became apparent that the group was in possession of countless firearms, old and new, all of which were fully capable of using live rounds. Some of these firearms were loaded to the max. Now, over the years I checked countless numbers of people in the bush with firearms of every sort and size, legal and illegal, so dealing with firearms was not an issue. However, it seemed that this group needed a bit of courage in the form of alcohol and drugs to make the experience more realistic or memorable or both. These guys were bombed, to say the least, and not from planes overhead. Once we realized just how much liquor the group possessed, how impaired some of them were, and how many weapons were in their possession, the hair on the back of our necks began to stand up. Needless to say, this group of guys was not in the same league as our true Canadian war veterans and heroes.

After seizing the drugs, liquor and illegal firearms and issuing some tickets, we managed to leave the group without incident. I often wondered though if any other unseen group members may have been watching us through a scoped "sniper rifle" from a distant vantage point.

Tree Planters

Tree planters love being in the bush, and it seemed to me that many really liked "getting back to nature." One day in Merritt, a call came in on a hot summer day of shots having been fired south of town toward Princeton. The complainant had been a worker from a tree-planter camp just off the highway a short distance. Had it been fall during an open hunting season, I probably wouldn't have attended, as hearing shots in the fall was a normal occurrence. However, being summertime, I felt that I had best head down and have a look around.

Directions in hand, I headed to the area, wondering what the day would bring. Following the directions, as I neared the road I slowed down and made my way off the highway and onto an old logging road. A short distance in, I could see an ATCO trailer in the distance, with a few tents scattered throughout the pines adjacent to the road. The front part of the camp area was on a bit of a side slope, and I slowed right down as I entered. Encouraging my truck along slowly, I suddenly noticed a tent beside the road to my left. Next to the tent was a man sitting cross-legged, stitching some type of leather object. The item he was repairing is dim in my memory because what really caught my attention was that the guy didn't have a stitch of clothing on—I'm talking buck naked, head to toe.

This was a bit strange, to say the least, but I pretended nothing was amiss, stopped the truck, rolled down the window, and asked the guy if someone in the camp had reported hearing gunshots. The guy looked up at me, never letting on that anything was out of the ordinary and said that he had not. He indicated that perhaps the gals across the road had heard something and pointed ahead of the truck and across the road. I thanked him, thinking that the whole thing was fairly weird, and rolled the truck slowly ahead.

Now I was looking slightly downhill toward a second tent and could just see the top of it a short distance ahead on the right. As the truck rolled slowly forward the tent came into full view, and there were the two gals all right, in exactly the same condition as the first dude, naked as jaybirds. There they were, stretched right out on blankets beside the tent, completely enjoying their time off. (Did I happen to mention they appeared fairly fit and healthy?) They glanced over at me and waved hello, and I managed to wave back feebly. As much as I needed to stop and talk to them, I simply didn't have the nerve. Yes, I'm one of those guys in high school that always had trouble working up the courage to ask a gal out for a date, and this situation seemed somewhat the same, that is, just plain awkward. So, I just drove slowly on past and avoided the entire situation.

As the sunbathers disappeared from view behind the truck cab (that's probably why I have neck problems to this day), a lone guy came walking out of the bush from the right side just ahead. He nonchalantly turned away from me and walked down the centre of the little road. He did have more items covering his hide than the gals—a lone towel draped over his right shoulder. Nothing weird about that, right? I was beginning to get the entire picture as to how this tree planter camp spent its time off in the bush. As my truck pulled up behind him, I saw that he had walked out from a homemade hot tub, made from an old cast iron bathtub, set over hot coals. Actually, it was pretty ingenious I thought, probably a great way to soak the old bones after hoofing it through cut blocks all day. As he stepped aside, I stopped the truck and rolled down the passenger window, asking him about the shots. He indicated he didn't know anything but said that the boss's quarters were in the trailer just ahead. I just thanked him and moved on.

Getting out of the truck I went to the trailer and found the boss man, finally finding somebody with clothes on to talk to. He pointed me in the direction of the shots, and so I headed back out to the highway. As I passed the gals, they waved a friendly goodbye as if all was completely normal. I waved back and carried on.

I should mention I never did find the source of the shots that day and headed home empty-handed. But then again, did it really matter? I'd had enough entertainment for one day.

Yes, you never knew what you'd run into in the bush, be it devil worshippers, gun enthusiasts, back to nature-ites, Aryan-nation members, biker gangs or other gang members. Every day could be a whole new ballgame in the backcountry areas of BC for a CO, and often it was.

22

WE'VE GOT YOU NOW

There was the odd occasion when a bear complaint became personal and a test of ability. One coastal grizzly bear gave me a serious run for my money and taught me a thing or two about eating humble pie, more than once.

Grizzly problems were fairly rare in the Squamish area, but occasionally a grizzly would surface from seemingly nowhere and start running into conflict with rural property owners. In this particular case, a relatively non-aggressive grizzly began appearing on acreages in the upper Squamish valley, raiding gardens and loitering around homes, which tended to make the residents rather anxious ... for good reason. The lone bear was reported as large and tended to saunter through yards near windows, un-nerving the folks inside peering wide-eyed at the bear at seemingly close range.

Bears truly do have distinctive personalities. Some are easy going and rarely show aggression until pressed, while others simply want a piece of you as soon as they set eyes on you. Grizzlies are more aggressive than black bears; it's in their genetics. However, some grizzlies are definitely easier going and more tolerant of humans than others. An older male grizzly typically tries to avoid confrontation, unless he has killed or claimed a carcass, in which case that level of tolerance drastically reduces, and he will usually charge any intruder he encounters on the kill.

Sows seem to have a shorter fuse and tolerate humans less, likely because they spend a good portion of their lives protecting and defending their cubs from boars. Even lone sows can be grouchy without good reason. We didn't call them "grouchy bears" for nothing. Regardless, if you put yourself inside any grizzly bear's comfort zone, a charge will likely result. Dealing with grizzlies always meant taking extra precautions for our own safety and the people that the bear chose to cause problems for.

This bear had been non-aggressive to date but had a taste for fresh, tender carrots, and was making quick work of a big garden that had been nurtured throughout the summer. The thing that was hard for the complainant to accept was the huge manure piles the offending bear was leaving behind in the garden that consisted of nothing more than chewed up undigested carrots. Raiding the garden carrots was one thing but dumping them out the back end as fast as they went in the front end was rubbing the landowner the wrong way. If the bear was bound and determined to raid his garden, at the very least, the bear could put the carrots to good use.

The bear seemed to be bedding or feeding beyond a neighbouring rural property, located roughly half a mile down the highway. Folks residing there advised that on more than one occasion it had walked by their living room window, and then showed up at the neighbouring garden after that.

It was fall, and my partner, Shawn, and I surveyed the garden and surrounding area and found good-sized tracks left in the soft, tilled soil. We knew from the track size we were dealing with a large adult bear, and there had been no reports of cubs. As grizzly complaints in the valley were rare, we hoped we could catch the bear and relocate it if possible, but catching fall bears can be a challenge with the abundant food sources around. With winter just around the corner, bears consume a lot of groceries in the fall months; often, fall bear complaints were associated with a lot of food attractions like apples, gardens, or spawning and dying salmon, all those fall food sources that become ripe for the taking. The salmon were running in the river, and all the little side tributaries were alive with chums and pinks. With the abundance of food, our task was to make our bait more attractive than all the other food sources in the area.

The bear had been seen at one or two of the neighbouring residences, however, it's favourite hangout seemed to be the home with the large unfenced garden, wonderful carrots and small stream in the backyard. We advised the other neighbours of our intentions, and to contact us right away if the bear made any visits to their yards. As such, we looked the garden property over and decided on a big maple tree in the middle of a large opening perhaps sixty yards from the garden as our snare location. It would give us the ability to get our vehicle and the bear trap right to the site when we caught the bear, and more importantly, it allowed us a good field of view on approach.

When handling a snared grizzly, we always had to be careful with the initial approach, as we wouldn't know how long it had been in the snare. If caught at dusk or early evening, and the approach was not made until morning, a bear had all night to chew at the steel cable that held its leg. On approach, a snared grizzly will often charge, and the cable attached to the tree might be six feet in length. If the bear lies on the far side of the tree, it has a twelve-foot running start before it reaches the end of the cable. At that point, the cable must withstand the energy of a very large bear coming to a very abrupt halt. That may be all it takes for a chewed cable to snap and make things very interesting, very quickly. The good field of view was for safety purposes.

With the aroma of dead and rotting salmon wafting up the valley, we had no problem finding bait, and using brush, we constructed what we thought was a sure thing under the big maple. Though the bait was no more stinky than the salmon carcasses scattered throughout the valley, the grizzly would not be able to resist the odour when passing the maple tree enroute to the garden. Standing back we admired our snare cubby setup and envisioned the large bruin lumbering into the sweet-smelling maggoty fish carcasses without a care in the world, stepping over the front log, and falling victim to our handiwork. From there, we would have the easy task of evaluating the bear's condition for relocation purposes, darting it, removing the snare, manhandling it into the live trap, and driving it away to greener and safer pastures … No problem.

We chose to use the snare, as over the years I found grizzlies much more hesitant to enter live culvert traps. I knew COs who had success with culvert traps on dump grizzlies, but this was not a dump situation. The snare setup had a more natural appearance and tended not to put bears on alert. Although the snare spring and cable were not well hidden, bears and cougars were generally not spooked by the smell of steel cable or human scent. With the garden raiding grizzly as good as in the bag, we headed for home.

At first light, we were back, slowly working the pickup to within binocular range of the maple tree. Snared bears often lay still and may not show themselves until approached. However, the telltale sign that a bear may be caught is when the cubby brush is knocked over. Once captured, a bear will fight the cable a bit, and anything within the bear or cable's reach gets a rototilling. Straining through the glasses it became clear that something had been disturbed, but the main body of the cubby was still upright, leaning against the maple. Upon approach, it was clear that one side of the cubby had been pulled open. The culprit had reached in from the side and taken all the salmon without setting off the snare.

I'd experienced this same type of bear snare thievery with a large cattle-killing boar grizzly I'd attempted to catch in the Nimpo Lake Country in the late 1980s. That boar had given me a humbling lesson on bear snaring, as it had broken into the cubby and stolen the bait three times. It was as if it had been watching the setup and knew exactly how to go in through the side to avoid being caught.

Grizzly bear snare

OK, so the garden grizzly got lucky one night. No problem, we rebuilt the snare cubby, and this time we added much more brush on the sides, constructing it to Fort Knox standards. No grizzly was going to break in through the side and feed us humble pie again. Replenishing the bait with new salmon carcasses, I was sure we'd have the bear this time. It had come right in for the bait the first night, and once a bear gets a taste of something it likes, it will always come back.

Returning the following morning, we found the same result. The bear had pushed one side of the cubby aside, stepped in, and pulled out the bait. Okay, the gloves were off now, and this was getting personal. If we couldn't coax the bear into the front of a snare, there would be no choice but to destroy it if we found it in the open, as free-range darting a bear, especially a grizzly, was extremely dangerous and a non-starter. Darting a bear that was not up a tree, or in a snare or culvert trap was too risky. Too much ground could be covered by a bear once darted, and not being able to find a drugged bear once down was a real possibility. That had happened to me once before, and I was not going to risk it again, especially with a grizzly. Again, we repaired the snare and headed home, fully intending to come back at dusk to watch for the bear.

Returning at dusk, we settled in at the edge of the clearing for an evening in the pickup, taking turns watching for the bear's approach. It was dark now, and by nine o'clock that evening the grizzly had not appeared. We began to wonder why. Suddenly our mobile phone rang; the neighbour half a mile up the highway advised us that the grizzly was peering in their living room window right at that moment. We fired up the truck and roared up the highway, really not sure what we intended to do if it was still there, but we at least wanted to get a look at the bear we had not seen yet. Arriving, the excited resident relayed how the grizzly had appeared at his living room window but had disappeared after he had called us. Suddenly, Shawn and I looked at each other and were hit with the same realization that perhaps the bear was headed to its favourite garden spot and our maple tree.

Back into the truck, back down the highway and back to the big maple tree. We were gone perhaps five minutes, and there at the base of the maple was an empty snare, bait gone. We were incredulous. This grizzly had just out-maneuvered, out-flanked and undressed us in five minutes for the third time. It was unbelievable. Resetting the snare, we tucked our tails and headed for home and began brainstorming some guerrilla tactics to outwit this nervy bear. That night I didn't sleep much, and by morning had devised a plan that had to be foolproof. The bear's weak spot was the bait, and that was the answer.

With a "We've got you now" attitude, we drove up again in the morning, stopping along the way for some fresh salmon carcasses we found lying along a small stream and chatted with the garden owner about our plans. In the field not far from the maple tree, I dug a round, post hole as deep as I could reach with a shovel, roughly ten inches in diameter. It had to be just big enough for an adult grizzly to reach in with one front paw. Slopping the new salmon bait into the deep hole, I arranged the snare to sit perched against the outside perimeter of the hole just below ground level. The spring trigger was dug in and set below the snare cable in the hole so that when the bear reached into the hole, its entire paw would be well past the cable before touching the spring trigger. The snare was attached to a heavy log that would serve as a drag. As a finishing touch, a rotten fish head was placed strategically on the ground as an attractor near the new snare. There was no possible way it could outsmart us this time. Once again, the garden grizzly was as good as caught as we departed full of anticipation.

This was beyond personal now and getting ridiculous, and I knew I couldn't spend many more days doing this, as other work issues needed attending. However, grizzly-human conflicts were not something to be taken lightly, and I put the safety of valley residents at the top of my priority list.

To say this was a series of highs and lows is an understatement. The next morning walking up toward my fool-proof-hole-in-the-ground-sure-thing-never-miss snare, the large bear was nowhere in sight, but the drag log was still sitting right where we had placed it. The drag should have been missing along with the caught bear …right? Then it became clear that an object *was* actually missing … the attractor fish head … strange. Peering into the vacant hole with dumbfounded expressions, we could see all the contents had been removed, and the snare cable was neatly flopped on the ground just off to one side. The trigger had been sprung; however, the cable had been lifted off first. It was as though the bear knew exactly what the snare cable was, snagged it with a claw and laid it aside, then set off the spring and took the bait. This bear had to have been caught previously. Deflated and nearing our wits' end, it struck me again though, that the bear's weak spot was the bait. It loved the fish we were laying out for it every night.

As such, a final plan that took the hole-in-the-ground routine to the next level was hatched. The hole was replenished with fish. The snare was reset. However, thirty feet from the snare hole was an old chicken coop with an old window-opening facing the snare. The fish head was again set out as an attractor, but I placed it between the snare and the chicken coop. Attaching a string to the head, I ran the string through the opening into the coop.

It seemed this bear would not be caught, and although I supposed we could have continued the same relocation game for an additional week, this had to end. Every day that went past without removing the bear was another day the folks in the area were at risk of a dangerous bear encounter. Unfortunately, it was more likely now that the bear would have to be destroyed unless the snares did their job.

After dark that evening we returned, yet again, and as we entered the site, there, just across the little stream a stone's throw away behind the maple tree, was a set of gleaming green eyes in our headlights, peering through the darkness at us from just inside the bush line. Stopping the truck, I threw the binoculars up, but they only revealed the bright glowing eyes, nothing more. It had to be our bear, no doubt about it. It appeared that we had arrived just as our nemesis was contemplating coming in for the evening. I considered doing the rifle deed right then and there, but the risk was far too great on a number of fronts.

Parking the truck while keenly aware that a large grizzly was out there in the dark very close by, we advised the garden owner of our plans and entered their chicken coop. The coop was blacker than the inside of a cow, but a dim light shone out across the opening toward the maple tree from the porch light on the house about fifty metres behind us. That light scarcely illuminated the area. Right inside the window opening, Shawn held a spotlight at the ready, while I gently held the string tied tight to the fish head with my left hand. In my right hand, I held my .338 rifle. With mixed feelings, I knew this complaint had to come to an end tonight as we knew the grizzly would come in for the bait and garden again. If the bear went directly to the ground snare and was caught, we were prepared to dart and immobilize it then and there. If the bear picked up the fish head that we had placed between us and the snare, it probably would mean the bear had pulled out the snare again, emptied the bait hole and was now taking the head as dessert. I was attached to the other end of the string, and the motion would be transferred to my hand. At that point I would simply say "OK" to Shawn, he would hit the light, and my rifle would end the complaint.

We stood motionless in the silent darkness for twenty minutes, knowing full well a large grizzly was nearby on the far side of the lazy little stream. As we continued to wait, it became apparent that something was keeping the bear from coming in. Was it our scent? Did it know we were there? Just how smart was this grizzly anyway? We scratched our heads in the dark, then realized the problem might be the porch light on the house illuminating the yard, and it needed to be turned off. Shawn drew the short straw and made a stealthy fifty-yard dash across the garden and over to the house to shut off the light. I knew Shawn felt more than a little exposed out there, but then again, he appreciated all the field experience he could get (at least that is how I justified it to myself). Relieved when he successfully made the tense dash back from the house in the dark, he re-entered the chicken coop with me. Once again, we took up our positions, and not one minute later heard the tell-tale cracking and crunching of a large animal approaching from the far side of the stream. The light had been the problem and the garden grizzly was coming in.

Knowing we were in it up to our eyeballs now, my right leg began to shake as the adrenaline started making its way through my system. Cussing silently, I told myself to settle down and concentrate on the string tension. Shawn was dead quiet. The crunching and snapping of brush changed to the slopping of water as the grizzly crossed the little stream about sixty metres away. Then, all went silent. It struck me right then that I hadn't thought about the grassy clearing that would provide a completely silent approach for the bear in the dark. Again, I cussed myself big time. All we knew was that the big grizzly was out in front of us somewhere in the pitch-black opening, perhaps standing motionless testing the night air with its big black nose that likely resembled the business end of a double-barreled shotgun. Or perhaps it was simply strolling toward the bait. Or perhaps it was already behind us making its way to the garden.

Regardless, the fish head attached to my string was on our side of the ground snare, and the bear had to come past the snare to get to it. We would only have one chance, and that would be if the bear was immediately in front of us at close range when Shawn hit the light. If we hit the light too soon and the bear was not right there, we would likely lose our chance. We also weren't sure what the bear's reaction to the light at close range would be. I did know our wives wouldn't approve of us putting ourselves within twenty-five feet of a big grizzly in the dark, but I was more worried about the two of us and the bear at this point.

The silence was deafening. Then I felt a bump on the string. I don't recall how I alerted Shawn, but he hit the spotlight and I released the string while raising my rifle, fully expecting the bear to be right in front of us and for all hell to break loose. There in front of us … was absolutely nothing … nothing at all. A string with a fish head still tied to it lay there, with no grizzly attached to it. No bear, no noise, no nothing. What the heck? Talk about extreme highs and lows in the span of ten seconds!

Slowly our spiked adrenaline started to come down, and we could only surmise what had happened. We believe the bear had made its way to near the bait site, then must have caught our scent, or perhaps saw us blindly peering out the opening into the darkness like a couple of terrified dummies. Whichever occurred, it bolted silently across the grass in front of us in the dark, stepping on the tight string with one paw as it ran past. In the one second it took to alert Shawn and turn the spotlight on, the bear had already passed across in front of us, out of our field of view, and was gone into the darkness. What amazed us was the silence of the whole affair. There hadn't been so much as a sound once the bear left the creek. It was amazing.

This story had a sad ending though, as a week or so later the bear showed up at another rural residence nearby and was shot on sight by the landowner. Other than the night we saw its glowing green eyes peering back at us in the darkness, we never set eyes on the bear until we were notified about its death and drove up the valley to pick up the bear's body. The grizzly was a large male silver tip that wore numbered ear tags in both ears from previous times it had been caught and relocated. It had been relocated by helicopter into Knight Inlet, 350 kilometres away, on two previous occasions and had made its way back to Squamish. Our suspicion about the grizzly having had previous dealings with snares and humans was correct.

Although this type of unfortunate ending is more common than not for relocated problem grizzlies, I still held a great deal of respect for this bear. It never did show any aggressive tendencies that I was aware of during its human encounters in the Squamish River Valley, or during any of our dealings with it. It had though, taught me a great deal about grizzly bear behaviour and intelligence.

23

MARRIED
TO THE JOB

Life as a Conservation Officer was always interesting and in many different ways. The investigations themselves were addictive, and the time spent working in the bush provided not only a form of solace for me but also afforded me the continual opportunity to enjoy nature. My role also provided another interesting sidebar throughout the years though, which many law enforcement people can likely relate to.

Shannon and I spent two and a half years in Merritt before we took a transfer to Bella Coola. We were newlyweds when we moved from Kamloops to Merritt and bought our first home there. In addition to renovating back porches and decks, building fences and planting a big garden, we also got our first dog there: Ben, a goofy black lab pup. All those activities, including learning my new CO job, filled our days. Therefore, we never really spent much time socializing outside the law enforcement community, except for getting to know our immediate neighbours.

When we moved to Bella Coola, however, it was easy to get to know people in the friendly small community. And although I worked alone, my office was located in the heavily staffed Forest

Service building. This gave us ample opportunity to meet and socialize with valley folks. That's when the phenomenon began.

The first time it happened, it really never occurred to us that it even had. Shannon and I were being introduced to a few people as "Keith, the conservation officer," and "Shannon, the game warden's wife." It did not seem that odd at the time, as we were new to the area, I was proud of what I did, and it was fair enough that folks ought to know who we were. As the years went by and we transferred around the province through various communities, we began to take note of this "handle" that always accompanied our introductions in non-enforcement circles. It would even happen to Shannon when I was not with her. Why did other people not get introduced with their working role in life? No one else got introduced with handles like "Joe, the commercial fisherman" or "Jane, the cattle rancher's wife." Those folks got introduced as Joe and Jane Smith, or Joe Smith and his wife, Jane. For Shannon and myself, it became a standing wink or nudge personal joke between us over my entire career.

The reason we were introduced that way was simple. Folks in the hunting and fishing community always liked to know who they were talking to, especially when game wardens or their families were within earshot. Most outdoor enthusiasts are law-abiding; however, many people have some sort of skeleton in their closet they like to keep locked away. It may be nothing more than a slightly illegal fishing experience, or a questionable hunting story their father told regularly, or perhaps a buck their brother shot that "wasn't quite legal." Whatever the reason, talking a little too freely in front of myself or Shannon was always safeguarded by the predictable name introductions. It tended to irritate Shannon more than me, in that she felt she was always "just the game warden's wife."

Of course, I would tease Shannon about it, and that she really should know her place in life as a "wife" and stand at least three feet behind me at all times. I was cagey enough not to be within striking distance of her when I said it though, and would run for cover squealing like a four-year-old, while she chased me around the house pounding me on the head with the nearest couch pillow. But seriously, I did appreciate her frustration over the years being married to my job.

Shannon also had to be a walking version of the Wildlife and Fisheries Acts. She would constantly field regulation questions from the hunting and fishing community and try to do her level best to help them out. However, she would end most conversations with, "You better talk to Keith about that one."

There was, however, a certain amount of etiquette associated with Shannon being partnered with a law enforcement peace officer. I, like all enforcement folks, had to maintain a professional lifestyle over the years, and as such, that applied to Shannon too. It was not hard to do, though, and becomes a way of life for law enforcement folks. We didn't hang out at the pub, act like idiots and stumble home drunk, or go to the river and bonk twenty fish. There were unwritten rules, and we followed them. But like I said, it was easy, as we didn't (and still don't) live our lives like that anyway.

Although the public spotlight on us over the years did prove "interesting" and was provided completely free of charge, at times it *was* an unfortunate cost of doing CO business I suppose.

24

HOME
FORENSICS

The bull moose population in the Peace Country had been slowly but steadily declining over a ten-year period prior to 1996. The Wildlife Branch knew they had to do something to stop this trend and came up with a number of possible management remedies involving hunting regulations. The decision was not easy for them, as they had several factors to consider, including the needs and wants of the guide-outfitters and the needs and wants of the resident hunters. Some of the options included limited entry seasons, bag limit quota changes and antler-size restrictions. After much debate, the antler restriction option was chosen, albeit we (the COs) knew it would likely result in an increase in illegal kills due to antler misidentification, whether intentional or not. Looking back though, the antler restriction did allow more overall bull moose survival in the Peace area in the years following. Unfortunately, just as the bull numbers were recovering, the moose population took a major winter-die-off hit in 2006 and has not been the same since. In fact, despite our wildlife managers best efforts, the moose population has experienced a general decline province-wide for the past four decades.

The antler restriction initially required that only bull moose with no more than two points on one antler (a yearling) or a minimum of three points on the brow palm on at least one antler (a mature bull) could be harvested. This offered the mid-aged breeding bulls some protection, resulting in more cows being bred. An additional requirement to the point regulation was that the antlers had to accompany the carcass. In other words, a hunter could not leave the antlers in the bush.

Some people made an honest mistake counting or identifying points for one reason or another and accidentally shot an illegal bull. Some of those folks called in their mistake, and some did not. Some would take the bull home anyway not wanting to waste it, and if not apprehended along the way, they avoided a fine and seizure. Then there were those folks (and I won't call them hunters) who killed a bull moose that "should have" been big (or small) enough to have the points required, or who simply didn't care. In other words, shoot first, count points second. The folks I am talking about are the ones who walked away from a bull moose they killed because it lacked the required points, then likely went on to do it again or until they finally killed a legal bull. I attended dozens of these cases after 1996, most of which were unsolved if there were no witnesses or suspects.

The fall of 1998 was progressing in a fairly average fashion, with numerous shot and left moose being reported, usually well after the fact. It was often only the presence of ravens and magpies squawking on a week-old carcass hidden in the bush that gave a moose kill away, and by then the culprit was long gone. However, one day I received a call regarding a fresh moose kill. In this case, the carcass had been taken, but the head bearing illegal antlers had been left in the bush at the kill site. It sounded to me like one of those cases where a bull moose bearing illegal antlers had been killed, but the hunter chanced taking it home anyway.

Hopping into the Dodge 4x4, I headed to the site near the Puggins Mountain Road, west of Dawson Creek. Raven activity had led both the complainant and myself to the moose kill in an open cut block. Ravens have unbelievable eyesight, and it does not take long for them to find a new food source. Following the directions, I easily found the moose remains in a new logging block in Rainey Creek. Moose are creatures of habit, and once the forested area they called home is logged off, they will often still pass through the open block, especially during the rut when the bulls are travelling and pursuing cows.

I could see by tire marks that the shooter had managed to get an ATV right to where the moose had fallen. There, the moose had been dressed out and loaded. The bull's head had been cut off with a saw a few inches back from its skull and left behind with the entrails. The bull was mature and had grown a large rack of antlers, however, the brow palms only possessed two points on each antler rather than the minimum three required by regulation. This was obviously why the antlers had been left behind. A search for any other evidence netted nothing, so I took a few photos, loaded the moose head and antlers into the rear of my truck and headed out.

With no suspects, I thought about my investigative predicament as the heavily sprung three-quarter-ton 4x4 bounced along on the rough logging road. The kill had been made within the past day or so. Unless the person was from out of the area and immediately headed home, there was a chance of finding the moose meat hanging somewhere, with a little luck. But where to start was the question. The moose was a big mature bull and would have had a larger than average body size, so I knew I was looking for a big-bodied moose. With no empty shell casings left in the cut block to indicate the calibre of rifle used, or any other evidence tying any one person to the incident, solving the file seemed quite unlikely. Mulling over all the facts thus far, I was doubtful I would find the responsible party unless I managed to get lucky, or get an information break of some type.

Shot and left bull moose in Peace Country

Butcher shops were places I visited often looking for hunter information, as few hunters cut their own meat. Meat cutters who handle wild game are required to keep records that identify a hunter's name, address and date of kill. I felt I had a good working relationship with the Dawson Creek area meat cutters, and although I occasionally took business away from them by seizing a carcass as evidence, they understood that some animals were illegal and required seizure. They were usually very helpful both with information and physically handling the meat.

I stopped at the closest meat-cutting shop located in the Upper Cutbank on my way back to town and struck up a conversation with Carl, who ran his meat-cutting business out of a shop beside his farm home. Carl always welcomed me into the shop, where the coffee pot was always on and occasionally, his good wife would bring out cookies. We chatted about the fall in general and how things were going for him. He said it had been a pretty good fall for the meat-cutting business, and we chatted about the fall hunters' success. I asked Carl if he had had any moose come into

his shop in the past couple of days, and he said that he had. I asked if he minded if I had a look, so he led me into the walk-in cooler where the skinned moose carcasses were hanging.

Most of the time moose were cut into four quarters for handling purposes, and numerous front and rear quarters were hanging in the locker. Carl pointed out the two moose that had come in recently, and one in particular caught my eye as it was quite large. The front half had not been halved, but hung as an entire skinned front half, minus the head, which meant it was brought in that way. If Carl had butchered the carcass, it would have been quartered. Carl couldn't recall if antlers had accompanied that particular moose when it had come in, but that was not unusual. It was not his role to ensure hunters who killed a moose kept the antlers with the carcass as required. In this case though, it had been a large bull, and Carl would have likely remembered handling the large antlers. Therefore, it meant that the head had already been removed prior to arriving at Carl's, or he probably would have remembered.

Checking the hunter records I noted the person associated with the moose was a local man who I did not know, and it was recorded as a bull. Nothing seemed really out of the ordinary so far, but I did have a large-bodied bull moose hanging in a shop not far from the kill location that was brought in without a head. Might mean something, might not. I advised Carl of the issue with the moose I was searching for and noted the hunter's name for follow up. Then I wandered back to look at the front half of the moose hanging in the locker again.

Looking it over, I again noted that the front half of the moose had not been halved into quarters, leaving the neck portion still round and intact, not split down the middle. The head had been cut off with a saw, and had not been cut off with a knife between vertebrae or at the back of the head behind the ball joint. This was also not unusual, but the facts surrounding this moose were beginning to somewhat fit those of the head laying in the back of my truck. If in fact, this was the same moose, the cut vertebrae attached to the head in my truck should match the cut vertebrae on the neck hanging in Carl's shop. That is if no other vertebrae were cut off the neck before it was hung at Carl's.

It was a long shot, but I felt it was worth a try to see if perhaps the cut vertebrae matched. I went back to the truck and had a closer look at the remaining neck vertebrae attached to the skull, noting how the cut angle seemed similar to the one in the shop. The head and attached vertebrae had been cut off in a fairly straight 90-degree manner. This was also not unusual, but things were adding up.

At this point, I had no proof of wrongdoing associated with the moose hanging in Carl's shop, so I really had no grounds to seize it. In fact, I did not want to seize it if it was not the moose in question. Therefore, I asked Carl if I could remove an inch or two off the end of the neck of the moose in his shop for comparison. He said that was no problem and brought over his electric bone saw that he used to quarter carcasses. While I held the hanging carcass, he cut off the top two inches of the neck and vertebrae and handed it to me. The chunk of vertebrae closely resembled an extra-large hamburger patty with chunks of sawed-off bone mixed in. Walking back to the truck I tried to fit the vertebrae to the head portion, but it was difficult with the bulky hide and hair still attached to the head portion. I thanked Carl for everything and said I would be in touch about the moose hanging in his shop. I decided to continue the examination of the bones at the office warehouse.

I had a gut feeling that I might be on the right track with the moose hanging at Carl's but still had no real proof. But now I had another conundrum; any type of formal forensic bone analysis to match pieces of bone or saw marks would take a long time. I had sent dozens of bullets, casings and animal hair to the RCMP Crime Lab for analysis over the years with a lot of success. The lab had proven many cases for me and had been very helpful, but it understandably took time for the analysis results to come back. This was time I did not have in this case. I would have had to cut the remaining vertebrae off the moose head, then send it and the vertebrae from Carl's shop to the crime lab for possible matching, then wait for the results, which would take a couple of months. By then the moose in Carl's shop would be long gone, cut into hundreds of pieces and given to four different families and half-eaten. I might still be able to prove that the moose hanging in Carl's shop was the bull that was killed in the cut block, but I may not be able to prove who killed it. Then there would also have to be search warrants executed, and some or all the moose could go missing. Time was not on my side in this case. I needed to find out if the illegal moose in question was the bull hanging in Carl's shop quickly before it left his shop.

Before I questioned the hunter whose name was registered with the bull in Carl's shop, I needed to take a closer look at those cut-off vertebrae. If I could at least tell with some certainty that the bones came from the same moose, I would have something on which to base my discussions with the suspect hunter. Right then and there I decided to do a little home forensics with my moose samples. However, I still needed to check one other local meat-cutting shop for any possible suspect moose before the day was done. Finding no other moose that fit the circumstances, I finally logged in my exhibits and called it a day.

It was a busy time of year with moose season coming to an end and multiple open case files hanging over my head, but two days later when I had cleared my plate enough, I got back to my moose samples. I went back to the exhibit storage with a saw and bucked off the remaining neck vertebrae from the illegal moose head. I then cleaned off the excess meat and cartilage from both sets of neck vertebrae the best I could, ensuring I did not damage or mark the ends cut by the shooter. Vertebrae are complex and strangely shaped with protrusions overlapping each other. Thus, when vertebrae are cut at 90 degrees, multiple bone protrusions of two attaching vertebrae end up being cut off on either side of the cut.

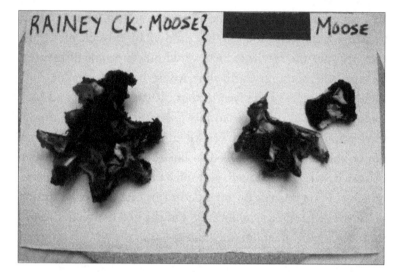

Vertebrae from illegal bull moose boiled and
forensically compared at home by Keith

Comparing the cuts, I still could not make a visual match due
to the amount of associated tissue attached and began to have my
doubts about them matching. I needed to rid the bones of some
of the meat and tissue, without the multiple pieces of cut bones
sloughing off into a mind-bending puzzle. It was time to start
cooking, so I took the bones home with me.

Back at the house, I convinced Shannon to let me use our
camp pots to cook the moose bones in. She reluctantly agreed,
after voicing her serious doubt about my plan having any possible
success. I explained to her that I had to try to get to the bottom
of this case quickly, or the file would likely get very long and
cumbersome.

I took some "before" photos of the two sets of neck bone
before setting them into separate pots of simmering water, and
ensured I knew positively which end cuts were mine and which
were the shooter's. With the aroma of simmering, rutting, moose
broth emanating through the house, I monitored the bones so as
not to over-cook them. Finally, they got to the stage where I could

pull the excess meat off, while the heavy neck cartilage remained, holding the bones together. Taking the bones out of the water, I immediately cleaned off the vertebrae as best I could, then set them aside to cool for a few minutes.

Each set of vertebrae held multiple bone pieces, big and small, and it was not a simple case of matching a couple of bones; there were many cut pieces. I picked up the two halves, placed the hunter-cut sides together and began rotating them in an attempt to match cut bones. I rotated the halves a couple of times and began thinking I held bones from two different moose. They just did not seem to match, even though the overall size was comparable. Then suddenly, while rotating the two halves for the umpteenth time, BOOM, there it was, the bone pieces fit together. I actually couldn't believe it, and I probably danced an Irish jig six times around the kitchen floor. They were a match, holy cow! Not that any court would accept my forensic evidence as an expert pathologist, but they matched nonetheless … and I knew the moose hanging in Carl's shop was the bull I was looking for … and I had a suspect's name. Life was good at that moment. I took "after" photos of the cooked bones then called Carl right away to tell him not to cut up the bull, and that I would be coming by to pick it up, unfortunately. He said no problem.

The next day I received a call from a local RCMP member who advised there was a hunter presently at their office who wanted to talk to me about a moose. Immediately, I headed over to the detachment and met the person. Low and behold it was the hunter whose moose had been hanging in Carl's meat locker. He advised he had called Carl's shop to see how the meat cutting was coming along, and was surprised when Carl told him that he could not cut up the moose because the game warden had a hold on it. I advised the hunter I already knew it was him who had tagged the bull moose, having matched the neck vertebrae. The hunter then fully confessed to shooting the bull and said that once he had spoken to Carl, he realized the jig was probably up. He stated he thought it had been a legal bull when he had shot at it, but when he walked up to it, he realized it was not legal. Rather than waste it, he took it and hoped he could get away with it. I did have to give him a little credit for not leaving it in the bush to rot.

The moose was not wasted, as I distributed the meat to a needy family. The hunter, on the other hand, was charged and fined for the offence. I took a lot of gratification in solving the case quickly and was more than a little happy with the results of my home-cooked forensics.

25

THE MEAT HOLE

As a conservation officer, problem wildlife was not the only issue I dealt with on a regular basis. Environmental law enforcement also formed a large part of my day-to-day duties. With a love and respect for the environment, including its fish and wildlife, I had little tolerance for resource abusers who took more than their lawful share of fish or wildlife, and there were many occasions when I discovered people in possession of too many fish for one reason or another. Over-limits were found under spare tires, buried in snowbanks, under gear, hidden in thermoses, stashed behind rocks and along trails, and of course in coolers or freezers.

The vast majority of anglers I met on the job, though, were law-abiding folks who respected the resource and were a pleasure to interact with. These people were always happy to see an officer in the field protecting the fishery resources. Most folks really enjoyed chatting and discussing the fishing and water conditions. This was actually a real fringe benefit of my CO work throughout the years. Having grown up fly fishing with Dad, we left Mom at home almost every weekend and took to the local lakes around Kamloops to flog the water. That love of fishing continues to this day. Anytime I have been able to discuss some of the finer points of angling or gain a little bit of insider information, it's been a real bonus.

I rarely let anyone with an over-limit leave without first issuing a fine, sometimes seizing their fishing equipment and in gross cases issuing a court appearance (Sister Mary, of course, was the exception). There were a few occasions with large fishing groups when a fish or two had been kept in error, perhaps resulting from a miscount by the group. In those instances, the extra fish were removed with a warning.

Anahim Lake is located in the west Chilcotin area, and the rainbow trout fishing there can be fabulous at times. The fish were generally not large, with most being in the range of twelve to fifteen inches. There used to be some wonderful days when a person could catch and release dozens of fish. I remember a fantastic day on the upper Dean River just downstream of Anahim Lake, when I managed to catch and release 100 rainbows on the fly. I stopped counting at that point. Sometimes when fishing was good, the temptation to keep extra fish was just too much for some folks.

The headwaters of the famous Dean River flows through Anahim Lake, and during the winter the rainbows begin congregating and preparing for spring spawning. The water is shallow, and the ice fishing was so good at times it was hard to believe. Where the Dean enters Anahim Lake it was locally known as the "Meat Hole", for good reason, for on some days as fast as a lure was dropped through the hole a rainbow would take the bait. On one winter occasion, I watched one person through my spotting scope pull, catch and kill twenty-five rainbows in less than an hour before they quit and were apprehended.

Given the quality of fishing in Anahim Lake, I regularly checked it for angling pressure during both the winter and summer months. I had a good rapport with a number of the resort owners in the area and would drop in to see how their fishing season was going, have a coffee and shoot the bull for a little while, and also do a cursory check of any clients who were in camp. I would check on other clients and anglers on the lake with my car-topper boat. The resort owners seemed to appreciate me dropping in occasionally, as it backed up their chats with clients regarding regulations and limits, and that they never knew when the game warden might show up and check for licences and fish.

Of course, the resort owners had a bit of a balancing act to perform when providing information about clients, as they were in the fish resort business and understandably wanted to "protect" their clients and their own reputation to a certain extent. No resort owner wanted to be known as someone who ratted-out every client that bent the rules a bit, yet they also needed and wanted to protect and preserve the future of their resort's fishing resource.

On a clear summer day, I pulled my truck into one of the Anahim Lake resorts and was greeted with the usual coffee, cake and Chilcotin hospitality. We visited for a while before the owner mentioned that I might want to check out a group of eleven people they had staying in their cabins who seemed to be catching a lot of fish. The group had been in for three days already. He went on to advise he had not specifically counted their fish but thought they had probably killed quite a number. He was being very diplomatic about it. Fair enough. I appreciated his dilemma, so I advised him that I would have a discrete check around the camp and not bring attention to the group by hot stepping from the office it to their cabins, demanding to see their fish. I suspected though, that he already had a pretty good idea of the actual fish numbers. I had no issue with him holding back a little though, and making me do a bit of fact-finding myself.

The daily limit at that time was six fish per person, and the possession limit was twice that, or twelve. Any children under sixteen did not require a fishing licence but could still catch their own limit of trout. That meant if all adults in the group were properly licensed and everyone was catching their own limit, they were allowed 132 fish when done, which was a lot of fish. Therefore, I was unsure of what I would find or how I might deal with it.

More often than not, most clients were out angling on the lake at midday, which now made finding and talking to them a bit of a challenge, but as I wandered through the resort and cabins, I found a few folks around. Knowing my target group's cabins, I casually made my way to them to see if anyone was there. Three ladies and three small children were present, so I struck up a conversation and asked how the group's fishing vacation was going, and how the fishing had been. They advised the fishing had been pretty good, and that the rest of the group was out on the lake fishing. I told them that was nice, then asked them where their fish were located, and they advised they were in the camp freezer. I had a quick check in their coolers at the cabins as standard procedure, found no fish, then asked them what the name associated with the group was and headed to the freezer.

Asking the camp owner to accompany me to the freezer building, we opened the large chest freezer and were greeted by dozens of bags of frozen rainbow trout, including other clients' fish. The bags were marked with client names, and we began counting out the bags, which appeared to contain roughly four fish each. When we were finished, the frozen fish count for the group was approximately 170 fish, well over their combined limit of 132. I thanked the owner and walked back to the cabin to talk to the ladies again.

At the cabin, I asked them for clarification on who was fishing and who was not. The ladies produced fishing licences but advised that the people out on the lake (their husbands) were the ones doing the fishing along with some of the kids. The numbers of who was catching how many fish were unknown; however, it seemed a number of the kids and wives were not keeping any fish. That lowered the 132 allowable trout number substantially, but I still really had no idea how many people in the group were actually fishing or keeping fish, therefore had no lawful trout total for the group. The cabin group comprised a number of families from the Lower Mainland on a group vacation, and they provided me with the names of the three men fishing with children out on the lake.

Launching my car-topper, I headed out on the lake to find the group along with anybody else fishing that day. After checking a couple of boats, I came upon a group of two men and a boy angling, and sure enough, they were part of the group. They advised the others were in a second boat across the bay, which they pointed out. All three were fishing, and I asked the men for their licences and also to have a look at any fish they had in the boat. Their licences were all in order, and they showed me seven fish that they had caught. I asked them if they would please go back to camp, as I needed to sort out their fish numbers. I then made my way to the second boat where I found the remaining man and one child, both fishing. Once again, I requested the same information, found five trout in their boat, and asked them to proceed back to camp.

There was now an additional twelve fresh trout, putting their total at approximately 182. It was an understatement that the group was over limit, but I hoped to ascertain who had caught what. Although it is not uncommon for people to catch a combined limit of fish, it is not legal, and anglers are only lawfully allowed to catch and retain their own limit of fish. It appeared this was the road the group had gone down, but failed to stop. They had already caught and retained more than their combined possession limit of trout, and they were still fishing.

One man seemed to be the group's leader and spokesperson, so back at shore, I took him aside to have a conversation away from the children and other distracting family members. I advised him that I had counted their frozen fish and that a number of family members were not catching or even angling for fish. After a short attempt at trying to justify all the fish, he finally relented and admitted that the three men and only a few of the kids were actually fishing. He admitted they were catching and killing too many trout but said they had never experienced fishing so good before, and just couldn't help themselves. He could not tell me how many trout each of the anglers in the group had retained, having lost count a long time before my arrival.

I concluded that only six people seemed to be angling in the group, which allowed for a total possession of seventy-two trout. Though the bags of fish were difficult to accurately count due to being frozen, the anglers had killed approximately 182 rainbows including the twelve fresh fish, putting them approximately 110 trout over-limit. Who caught how many fish on any given day was impossible to calculate, and at that point, it really did not matter.

Returning to the cabin, I spoke with the group's adults as a whole about the predicament, and they seemed to understand, although some were not too happy about the prospect of fines and seizures. I advised them that this was gross over-limit and that they ought to be setting a better example for their children about how to treat the natural resources. I think that struck a chord with them, and likely did more good than the tickets and fines I left some adults with. Their response to me was good, therefore a court appearance did not seem necessary. Not wanting to entirely ruin their vacation, I seized all fish in excess of their limits, along with a few rods and reels. I then advised them that they were now officially finished fishing and would have to enjoy the remainder of their holiday doing other activities.

They advised that they had planned to leave the following day anyway, therefore it was not too much of a hardship on them. I thanked them for their cooperation and hoped they had learned from their mistakes. Then I dropped in at the resort office to advise of my actions. The owners thanked me for being fair with the group, and I headed home somewhat satisfied that I had protected the Anahim Lake fishery resource at least a little bit that day.

26

THIS GRIZZLY CLIMBED

Over the years I was involved in many wildlife investigations that resulted in serious injuries to both animals and people. This book is not intended to focus solely on these unfortunate incidents; however, I did take a keen interest in serious wildlife occurrences during my career. Bear maulings were one of those scenarios that I had to deal with. I always used the information I gathered about bear behaviour during the attacks to educate myself and other people.

One of the maulings I investigated involved two young men who were very badly injured. The bear behaviour in this case was different than any other attack I had dealt with previously. The grizzly bear had climbed a tree. It is generally well-known that grizzlies cannot climb trees very well due to their large size and long claws. The following information was gathered from the numerous people I interviewed who were associated with the attack, as well my on-site investigation:

This incident involved a group of seismic workers in a sub-alpine mountainous area of the Red Deer River south of Dawson Creek in the summer of 1994. The group had been dropped off by helicopter on a steep mountainside and were in the process of laying out seismic cable on a recently cleared narrow seismic line at timberline. The crew did not typically carry firearms. They usually packed bear (pepper) spray for bear defence. On this day the group was required to exit the helicopter while it hovered with only its front struts contacting the hillside. As such, the tail section storage compartment could not be reached, and their gear containing their pepper spray had to be left behind. Whether or not that played a role is unknown.

The group was spread out along the seismic line over approximately 200 metres. Mark was out front, Adam was behind him by 100 metres, and the remainder of the group was behind Adam another 100 metres down the line. While laying out cable, Mark suddenly encountered a sub-adult grizzly bear at approximately thirty metres and it immediately charged him. Mark instinctively threw up a leg in self-defence, and the grizzly grabbed him by that leg and took him to the ground.

Adam could hear Mark frantically yelling, "Bear, bear!" so Adam immediately climbed a tree alongside the line. The remainder of the group could also hear the yelling and climbed trees as well, while Adam radioed for the helicopter.

The bear heard or saw the others and proceeded to drop Mark and charge down the line toward Adam and the rest of the spread-out group. This gave Mark the opportunity to climb a thirty-foot alpine fir located on the side of the line. Previously, when the seismic line had been cleared by chainsaw, the tree branches had been removed on the lower portions of trees bordering the line. As a result, many trees along the sides of the line now had four to six-inch tree stubs. This made climbing for Mark and Adam easier, but also provided climbing aids for the bear. Mark quickly climbed about twenty feet up the nearest tree; however, the grizzly either heard or sensed him doing this. Therefore, it broke off its charge toward Adam and charged back up the line toward Mark. Adam could hear Mark's screaming getting more frantic, so he moved closer up the line to see if he could help somehow. He watched helplessly as the bear climbed up the tree below Mark, took hold of his ankle in its mouth, and pulled him out of the tree to the ground, once again mauling Mark on the legs.

Seeing there was nothing he could do for Mark, Adam climbed over twenty feet up his tree. The grizzly then left Mark on the ground and charged back down the line toward Adam again. Adam saw the bear go under his tree and thought it had run past and away, but suddenly realized it was coming up the tree after him. Once the bear reached him, it grabbed hold of one of his lower legs and tried to pull him from the tree while Adam frantically held on and kicked at the bear. It tried repeatedly to jerk Adam from the tree, but Adam held on with all his might. Finally, the bear simply let go of the tree and held onto Adam with its mouth. The weight of the bear was too much and pulled Adam backward out of the tree. They both fell over twenty feet to the ground, where Adam was knocked unconscious.

Getting no fight from Adam, the bear dropped him and charged back up the line to Mark, who had re-climbed the same tree a second time. Again, the bear climbed up and pulled Mark out using the same technique as it had on Adam, by letting go of the tree and using its weight to pull him out. For a third time, the bear badly mauled Mark on the legs.

Finished with Mark, the grizzly charged back down the line, grabbed the still-unconscious Adam by the shoulder and shook him. Getting no response from Adam it charged back up toward Mark, who was no longer able to climb and had hidden under low-hanging evergreen branches. Mark could hear the bear aggressively huffing nearby for a few moments, then it simply vanished. Shortly thereafter, the helicopter arrived and hazed the area, and the two men along with the rest of the group were rescued.

Mark's lower leg injuries were very serious from having been mauled relentlessly. Adam's legs were also severely scratched and bitten, and he had a four canine punctures on his shoulder where the bear bit him once, from likely shaking him and getting no response. Both Mark and Adam were fortunate to be alive.

My partner and I attended the mauling site and set snares for a week, but the bear was not seen again. There are many different scenarios and factors which lead to different types of maulings, however, the facts of this event were typical of a defensive/ aggressive grizzly attack. When the bear had encountered the men suddenly, it felt threatened and proceeded to defend itself by aggressively mauling both of them. Once the bear felt the threats were diminished, it left the area.

The thing I found abnormal about this attack was the multiple times the bear climbed trees to reach its victims, and the distance between the victims. From the second tree Adam had climbed, we picked grizzly hair at over twenty feet in height. That particular tree had very few chainsaw stubs to assist the bear in climbing, just regular limbs. From the description, the bear, in this case, was believed to be a smaller sub-adult, but heavy enough to pull Mark and Adam from their trees. The young bear's size and weight likely played a role in enabling it to climb.

Bear maulings are an unfortunate reality of life in the bush. I used this particular bear's behaviour to assist me in providing bear awareness information to the public. Although not always successful, pepper spray discharged directly into a bear's mouth at point-blank range can have an effect. Pepper spray may have helped in this case if the men had had it with them. However, they still would have needed the time and ability to get out the spray and use it, and often times grizzly defensive/aggressive attacks are over quick enough that the victim has no time to get the spray out. Also, all bears don't react the same when sprayed. We'll never know if the outcome would have changed had Mark and Adam been packing bear spray.

27

GREED

I was fortunate enough to work on a broad array of investigations during my career. Though I always enjoyed tackling serious, complex wildlife cases, the files that also ranked high on my priority list were people over-limiting on fish. Greed was their only motive.

In the summer of 1984, while at Island Lake near Merritt, a group of anglers tipped me off about another party of camped fishermen they believed were abusing the daily limit and using illegal gang trolls (a "willow leaf" rig consisting of multiple metal attractor spoons, often used with a worm for bait). Island Lake was well known at the time for producing very large rainbow trout, and managed as a "trophy fishery". Accordingly, specific size limits and gear restrictions existed to protect the fishery. The daily limit for rainbows was two fish, however, only one fish per day could be kept larger than fifty centimetres (twenty inches). If an angler had camped-out and angled for more than one day, the possession limit doubled to four fish, two of which could be over fifty centimetres. Only flies were permitted for lures (no hardware or bait).

After taking the report from the group of fly fishermen, who were more than a little upset at the people they had reported, I approached the suspect camp on foot in full uniform. As I approached through the trees, I made eye contact with the group, and three men immediately made a mad dash for their car-topper boat pulled up at shore. I couldn't believe it. They were trying to get into their boat and take off, and they darn near made it. I broke into a sprint and managed to get my hand on the bow of the boat, now in knee-deep water, and pull them back to shore. As I stood there soaking wet, I was in no mood to hear their dozens of lame excuses and lies about what the heck they were doing. I simply walked over to their cooler and flipped open the lid.

The cooler was loaded to the brim with large rainbow trout, well over their group's lawful twelve fish possession limit. I had no idea where they thought they were going to escape to in their boat, and how it could possibly have ended well for them. All the fish were in the camp, not in the boat, and they would have had to come back to shore at some point. I guess they just panicked when they saw my uniform and thought they had to get away somehow. I'm sure they had consumed some liquid courage beforehand which aided their brilliant escape plan. Emptying the cooler, twenty-eight large rainbow trout were counted, many over the fifty-centimetre length. These guys were way over their limit. Walking back to the boat, their rods were rigged with illegal gang troll set-ups as well.

Needless to say, *all* their fish and fishing gear were seized, and they spent the remainder of their "fishing" expedition camping until they worked up the courage to go home. It likely got worse for them when they arrived back home, as they would have had a fair bit of explaining to do to their better-halves as to why they had to go down to the courthouse to pay hefty fines. The group that tipped me off was really happy that I had come along that day, and that the greedy men had been caught red-handed.

Once again, I was very satisfied that I had apprehended people driven by greed and so deserving of being caught. As always though, it saddened me to see people out there abusing our wonderful resources.

28

CLOSE CALL

Working the night shift during the late fall deer season was a necessity at times in the Peace Country. Deer and moose frequented alfalfa fields at night and occasionally the temptation of searching in the dark for trophies became too much for some people. One cold November night, I fired up the work truck at 11:00 p.m. and headed out for patrol in the Groundbirch area. It was a beautiful crystal-clear early-winter night. The stars were out, and the temperature hovered around minus ten degrees Celsius. Six inches of powdery snow covered the ground. I never knew what I might encounter on a night shift, and this night was no different, but I had a feeling something interesting was going to happen.

We lived in Arras, west of Dawson Creek, so this night I headed west from home on the Puggins Mountain Road which would eventually pop me out on Highway 97 near Groundbirch. Most Peace Country roads are straight and form a grid pattern, usually running north, south, east and west. The gravel roads are generally well-maintained and wide enough for two vehicles to easily pass one another; however, most of the time people travelled down the middle when the road was clear. Because of the grid pattern, I was always able to cover a lot of country, and it made it easy to never take the same road twice. The straight roads also allowed a person to, on occasion, get their speed up a little too high when they were familiar with the area.

On this night, the road was covered in hard, compact snow, and I clipped along doing about sixty km/hour. I knew full well that if a moose or deer suddenly stepped out onto the road and I had to brake, I would likely go into a slide. In any event, I kept my ditch lights on and my eyes open for animals and made my way west. No one was out and about, and the road was as empty as a ghost town.

I neared the crest of a hill that I knew dropped sharply away on the other side. The roll of this particular crest was not gradual, and the pitch changed suddenly onto the steep hill. It was a blind crest that allowed for no vision past the top of the hill. This was not usually a big deal, but tonight was different. As I approached the crest I had probably let off on the gas a little bit simply out of habit, but my speed was likely still right up there as I neared the hill. I have to admit, my old work truck was probably crowding the middle of the road a little bit too. But there was no traffic, right? Wrong. As I crested the hill, I found myself staring into the headlights of a car parked right in the middle of the road. I recall something to the effect of "Holy shit!" emanating through the cab as I hit the binders and swerved hard.

You know how the high school physics teacher always said that for every action there is an equal and opposite reaction? Well, when I hit the brakes and cranked the wheel on that slippery road, my truck immediately acquired a hard case of inertia and took matters into its own hands. Things happened fast, yet looking back, it is like it happened in slow motion. The truck swapped ends 180 degrees, and I recall seeing a person standing at the front of the car looking at me as I sailed past their driver's door at about fifty kilometres an hour in reverse. With my white knuckles squeezing every drop of life out of the steering wheel, I held on for dear life and prepared for sudden rear impact with a boulder, ditch, telephone pole or any other solid truck-wrecking, report-worthy object in the ditch.

Keith and new work pickup around the time of the "close call"

Amazingly, none occurred. The encounter had by chance taken place in the long span between two hydro poles, and the wide road allowance was clear with just a slight slope toward a shallow ditch. My truck came to rest, stalled in a rear-facing position without a mark on it, about 100 yards down the hill past the parked car. I was stunned. I couldn't believe both vehicles had come out of the incident unscathed, and that my undies were still clean.

Immediately, I was incredulous that someone would park a vehicle in the middle of a very slippery, icy country road at eleven o'clock at night in the pitch black, but there it was. Once the anger subsided though, I quickly realized how lucky we both had been, and that I had also been part of the problem. I fired up the truck and pulled up to the rear of what I could now see was an old Valiant car. Standing beside it was a lady who appeared to be very shocked by the incident, and I quickly got out and abruptly asked her what she was doing there. I tried to be nice, knowing that I was also in the wrong for going a little fast for the conditions, however, it's likely my adrenaline was still pumping a bit when I blurted out the question. She advised me she had almost made it up the hill but had spun out just shy of the crest and was now scared to move the car because it was so slippery.

Being hard and compact, the snowy winter road was indeed very slippery. However, as I shone my flashlight on the car's tires, I could see they were completely bald. I told her that we had to get both our vehicles off the road right away to avoid having another "holy shit" moment that might not end as favourably. She agreed and asked right away if I would move it for her.

She was obviously rattled and visibly shaken by what had just occurred, so I agreed. I quickly pulled my truck off to the side of the road, then piled into the old Valiant and tried to back it down the hill. It was a quarter-mile or so to the bottom, and I stepped on the brake and put the shift lever in neutral, hoping to slowly ease it back down the hill to a safer stopping point at the bottom. I gingerly attempted to nurse the brakes to control the rearward descent, but the car immediately went into a four-wheel slide. Now, here I was in the second out-of-control reverse vehicle slide in a matter of minutes. … Great, just great. Once again hanging on with white knuckles, I rode that old Valiant backward all the way down the hill in the dark in an out-of-control slide. I finally slowed near the bottom, where I spun it around and pulled it over to the side. Fortunately, it never slid off the roadway and all was well. Once stopped, I stepped out and called her down the hill, advising that it was okay now but to be really careful as it was very slippery to walk on.

When she reached the bottom of the hill, we had a conversation about what had transpired. She had been going over to a friend's house who did not live far from where we were. I politely scolded her about the condition of her tires, and that the car really had no business being on the slippery winter roads with tires in that condition. I did not want to see her get hurt, or hurt someone else for that matter. She sheepishly agreed and said she would drive her car back home slowly, with me following for safety. She got into the Valiant and slowly pulled out and headed for home, while I followed along for the mile to her driveway. Once I knew she was home safe and sound, I headed westward again for the remainder of the night.

Though I encountered no illegal hunting activity, that night still sticks in my mind to this day. I can't believe how lucky we both were to have come out unscathed. I had learned a valuable and humbling lesson about driving slippery winter roads that night. You just never knew what you might come up against during those winter night patrols in the Peace Country.

29

BUCKET HEAD

I t was quiet on a sunny mid-summer day in the Peace when a call from a rural school-bus driver came into the Dawson Creek office. The driver reported seeing a bear wandering along a gravel road with a bucket stuck on its head. I got the location description and chuckled to myself wondering how the heck the bear had gotten itself into such a predicament. Bears live by following their noses, and there was no doubt that whatever had been in the bucket had attracted the bear, and that the bucket had then somehow affixed itself to the bear's head.

The location was ten kilometres out of town, down past Pouce Coupe (a small community just south of Dawson Creek), so I headed out to the location with my tranquillizing equipment. I hoped to get the bear into a position where it would be safe to dart it and solve the problem. Stopping in the middle of nowhere, really, where the driver said he had spotted the bear, I shut the truck off and wandered around to have a look. The area seemed to be an old pasture, with a lot of willows mixed in with mature pine trees. The bush was pretty thick, so spotting anything at a distance was near to impossible. As I stood there pondering how the heck I was going to find a bear in the middle of nowhere with a bucket on its head, I heard a hollow "bonk." Turning toward the noise I stood quietly and listened, and about fifteen seconds later there was another resounding "bonk." The "bonking" continued about every thirty seconds. It sounded as though someone was hitting an empty five-gallon bucket against something solid, so I began to follow the "bonks."

About 100 yards from the road, I came across the strangest bear sighting I had ever encountered. There, ten yards in front of me was a small brown-phased black bear walking in a thirty-foot circle with an unopened five-gallon bucket firmly planted on its head. Every so often, it would walk blindly into a pine tree and a resounding "bonk" would echo through the quiet forest. Shaking my head and muttering to myself, "You've got to be kidding me!" (which, working alone, I tended to do quite regularly), I couldn't help but choke back a laugh, not wanting to startle the little guy.

That little brown bear had gotten himself into quite the predicament. Somehow, it had chewed and bored a small hole through the side of a plastic five-gallon-fish-fertilizer bucket, then forced its head through the hole to get at the contents. The edges of the hole had pushed inward, so when he tried to pull his head out, he was firmly trapped. The little guy had no doubt snuck into one of the neighbouring farms in the area, found a garden shed, and committed the deed. He looked like a furry brown hammer wandering around in the bush, completely blind, bouncing off trees. The bucket had a sealed lid on it. If it was not removed, the bear would eventually succumb to stress, exhaustion and suffocation.

Tranquillizing free-ranging bears was dangerous. It was usually a non-starter for me, due to the risk of a bear running off with a dart in it, then going down where I could not locate it. Or, the bear could pull the dart out and lose it, creating a stepping hazard. However, in this case, the risk was minimal due to the bear's predicament and inability to run successfully. ... And if it did bolt, I could follow the "bonks." Returning to the truck, I gathered up the darting equipment and made my way back to the bear. After a few minutes and a couple cc's of Telezol, the little guy was resting peacefully.

Brown-phase black bear with head stuck in a five-gallon-fish-fertilizer bucket after being tranquillized

The hole the bear had chewed in the bucket was barely big enough to allow the bear to force its head through, and the edges of it were very tight around the bear's neck and throat. That made it difficult to cut the bucket off without injuring the bear. The plastic on those buckets is quite tough, and I had to lean on my knife pretty heavily to cut through it. Finally, after managing to work the bucket off, I examined the bear. He seemed no worse for wear, and I found that he actually was a "he." Amazingly, he was not cut, so I placed a small numbered plastic ear tag on him and sat back to monitor his recovery.

Half an hour later he slowly came to. Like most recovering bears, he lay with only his head up for the first five minutes, then attempted to stand up on wobbly legs. After a few ungainly attempts, he unsteadily lumbered off into the brush away from me. Once again, I shook my head in disbelief and doubted I would ever encounter another bear in the same predicament. Over the years I never did.

30

NICE GUYS FINISH LAST

The winter of 1986 marked three years into my CO career, and on this particular day that winter I was riding a noisy, smoky snow machine down the cold and remote Blackwater Road north of Anahim Lake. The Anahim Lake RCMP and I were making our way, with a search warrant in hand, toward a property where a moose that had been shot during the closed season was supposedly located.

This investigation had started two days earlier when an informant advised me that a moose had been shot way down the Blackwater Road by two individuals, one of whom was well known to me for illegal hunting activities and for selling moose meat. The information seemed credible given the amount of detail and the description of how the two people had split the moose. One half had been brought out to Anahim Lake, where it vanished, and the other half had been left at one of the suspect's residences down the Blackwater Road.

With the information in hand, I attended the local Justice of the Peace in Anahim Lake and obtained a search warrant for the suspect residence and associated outbuildings. As I mentioned earlier, search warrants were much simpler to obtain back in those days, with less detail required to satisfy a JP's requirements.

The Dean River flows north out of Anahim Lake, and the Blackwater Road parallels the Dean many miles before the river turns west, gains volume and heads downhill to the central coast Dean Channel. Back in 1986, the road was an unmaintained "bush road," barely passable during summer months depending on how wet or dry the summer season was. During winter months the road was not plowed, so snow machines were needed to access homes or cabins there.

It was thirty or forty kilometres to the suspect's house, and finally, we arrived mid-morning. We kept a close watch for any sign of blood in the snow, but not having come across a kill site, and having no information about where it was actually located, we really didn't expect to see any sign enroute. Once close to the house though, we thought we might see some blood in the snow somewhere. If the moose had been towed by snow machine and toboggan, it would be very hard not to leave even a small amount of frozen blood mixed with snow somewhere on the white ground where it was off-loaded.

As we approached the front door, we could see snowmobile tracks here and there, but no blood or hair. Knocking on the front door a pleasant middle-aged man opened the door, and we identified ourselves. I advised the man we were looking for a moose that was supposedly brought there by two men. I named the suspects to him, as one of the suspects owned the house. He invited us inside the front door and advised he was just caretaking the home for the owner and had no idea about any moose. He seemed sincere and believable, and I advised him we would like to have a look in the garage and outbuildings, as we had a search warrant. He said no problem, and we began looking around the property.

Normally moose quarters are hung and stored in buildings separate from the living quarters, and in this case, there was a garage and a shed out back. We opened the garage, fully expecting moose quarters to be hanging there, but upon looking in, no sign of moose was found—no blood on the floor, no hair, no old ropes or meat hooks hanging vacant, nothing. We found the same in the other outbuilding as well—nothing. Having a careful look around the outside of the home, there was no sign of blood or any other evidence that might indicate portions of a moose had been off-loaded or moved in the vicinity of the house. We were puzzled, but perhaps our information had actually been wrong for some reason.

Although I possessed a warrant that allowed the residence itself to be searched, I saw no reason to actually enter the house and search it, due to the lack of any evidence outside. The caretaker seemed credible, and I felt we didn't need to push the issue and go through the house. When executing residential search warrants, I always tried to be as non-intrusive as possible. I tried to be decent with folks unless they gave me unnecessary or excessive grief. I only searched what I felt really required searching based on evidence, even though I had the lawful right to conduct an exhaustive search. Given what we did not find, we thanked the caretaker, got on our snow machines, and headed off down the snowy trail.

We dropped in at a few more homes along the road and made general inquiries but found no evidence of wrongdoing, so we made the long, cold ride back to the village of Anahim Lake empty-handed. Hot coffee and homemade cookies at the RCMP detachment felt really good after a long day on the noisy snow machines, but we were still puzzled by our lack of findings. Unfortunately, no further information ever came in about the moose, and the case went cold, as many "closed season" files did over the years.

Fast forward fifteen years to 2001, during my second posting in Bella Coola. While out at one of the local Anahim Lake ranches on unrelated business, I had the opportunity to speak with a fellow driving a team of horses and wagon. I did not recognize the man at first until we got chatting about life in the Chilcotin. He advised he had been the guy caretaking the suspect's house back in 1986. At that point, my memory of that day slowly started to de-fog, and I remembered him from that cold February day down the Blackwater.

Suddenly he simply said to me, "You know, Keith, you just didn't ask me the right question that day."

I instantly froze in my tracks, my mind started reeling and I began to get a heavy feeling in my gut. "What do you mean?" I said.

"Well," he added, "I was kind of in a bind that day, you know, caught between a rock and a hard place, being that I was caretaking the house and all, and you just didn't ask the right question."

"And what was that?" I instinctively knew what was coming next but did not want to actually believe it.

"Well," he continued, "you never asked me if the moose was actually in the house. You were standing twenty feet from it. It was around the corner lying in the kitchen just out of sight."

At that point, I must have reacted like someone who had just been struck by lightning. I was absolutely stunned, glazed over, and could barely mutter a coherent response.

He went on, "If you had asked if it was in the house, I would have told you and showed it to you, but you never asked. What was I supposed to do? The moose had been dropped off by those guys, I had nothing to do with it, and there I was caretaking the place, in possession of an illegal moose, and you and the Mounties show up. All I could do was ride out the situation at the time and hope for the best."

If at that point he told me what actually happened to the moose after we had left on snow machines that day, I don't recall, because I was simply too dumbfounded to remember any conversation after that point. How or why there had been no blood anywhere around that home back in 1986 is a mystery. All I know is that the old saying "Nice guys finish last" is true ... sometimes!

31

TOO CLOSE
FOR COMFORT

S hannon, the kids and I took two postings to Bella Coola with thirteen years in between. We truly enjoyed our times there. During our first posting in the 1980s, cougar complaints were fairly rare in the valley, but in the late 1990s, the cougar population had increased dramatically, resulting in continual cougar/human conflicts. The valley had also experienced a real decline in blacktail deer, indicative of high predator numbers

It was mid-winter in 2000; we had successfully survived the Y2K turn of the century, and there was three fresh inches of snow on the ground. Brycen and I were getting set to do a bit of exploring in the upper valley area. At 6:00 a.m. we gathered our lunch and gear and prepared to leave the house while it was still dark. Our driveway paralleled the Saloompt Road for seventy metres, and as we drove out toward the road, we noticed what appeared to be a drag mark across the driveway in the fresh snow.

Getting out of the pickup with the flashlight, I briefly studied the bloody drag and assumed by the tracks that a dog had dragged itself across the driveway. Following the drag mark to the edge of the yard under a tree, I found and recognized the neighbour's medium-sized border collie, quite dead, unfortunately. It had been a really friendly collie, but I knew that it had been getting old and hard of hearing. Retracing the drag back across the driveway and toward the road, I found a bloodstain where it appeared to have been struck. It seemed likely that it may not have heard a vehicle coming down the road and got hit. Back in the truck, I told Brycen what had unfortunately happened, and that we would go over to the neighbours' and tell them about their dog when we got back around lunchtime. It was still too early to go over to their house at 6:00 am.

Brycen and Nicole with female cougar that killed neighbour's dog

When we returned later that morning, we hadn't been home twenty minutes when the neighbour's daughter knocked on the door. She was inquiring around the neighbourhood if anyone had seen their dog. I explained to her as delicately as possible what had happened, and asked Brycen to take her over to where we had seen her dog lying to identify it. I told them I would be coming out right behind them as soon as I got my coat on. Looking back, I guess that was a little harsh, but the kids were used to seeing animals in all kinds of living and dead conditions with my job. Just as I headed out the door, Brycen came sprinting back to the house out of breath and blurted, "Dad, the dog's gone!" That information struck me like a hammer, and I told the kids they'd best get in the house while I went over and checked things out.

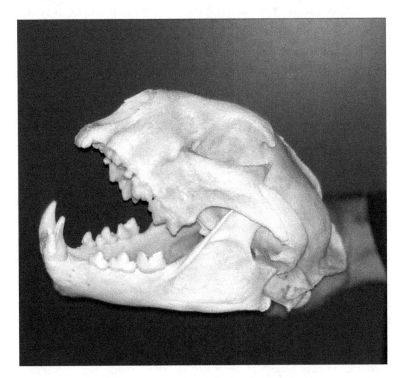

Skull from cougar that killed neighbour's dog.
Note broken and missing upper canine teeth

The collie was gone all right, and something had moved it. Taking a much closer look at the drag mark now, it was clear in the daylight that the tracks had not been made by the dog. They were cougar tracks. In the dark that morning, I had not taken the time to properly study the tracks, and at first appearance, they looked like dog tracks. I just assumed they were made by the collie dragging itself over to its final resting place. It was a good bet that the cougar had been very close by when I walked over to the dog in the dark, and in fact, our truck had probably moved it off the dog.

The cougar had jumped the collie on the road, killed it, dragged it off the road across our driveway and into our yard. Following the new drag mark and tracks in the snow for 150 metres, I found the dog once again. This time though it was clear to see a cougar had been the culprit, as all the hair had been licked off one side. It was odd though, that the cougar had not fed on it. So I quickly headed back to the house, grabbed my rifle and Brycen, and we returned and sat near the collie until it was dark. However, the cat never returned before dark that evening.

The next morning, I called David, the local hounds-man, and after a brief explanation of the circumstances when he arrived, we set off following his dogs up toward the base of the mountain. It was steep climbing through the big mature fir trees and Volkswagen-sized boulders that had careened off the mountain centuries earlier. After fifteen minutes we caught up to the dogs, but now they were wandering aimlessly among the trees and randomly baying. As usual, I took that as my cue to start looking up. There, thirty metres away, crouched among a cluster of fir boughs, staring intently at us was the culprit, a medium-sized cougar.

It was an old female with both top canine teeth broken off at the gum line. Due to her dental problem, she had likely taken to preying on easy targets, like easy-going, deaf old dogs rather than her normal prey, deer. The entire incident made me appreciate just how close a cougar can be without a person ever knowing it.

32

LADDER WORK

Tumbler Ridge is a small, picturesque community on the eastern edge of the Rocky Mountains in the BC Peace Country. It came to life in the early 1980s when coal mines were opened in the area. During my first posting in Merritt at that time, I recalled hearing about the bear problems associated with the mining camps that housed the workers building the infrastructure for the new coal mines. Like many towns that come to life, Tumbler Ridge underwent growing pains associated with wildlife. Nowadays though, those problems are not as prevalent, and Tumbler Ridge is a self-sufficient, small town that is a pleasure to visit.

Tumbler Ridge was within the Dawson Creek CO boundaries, and over my nine-year stint in Dawson Creek, I spent many days attending various wildlife complaints, patrolling and investigating files in and around the quaint community. There were never too many bear complaints, but occasionally a problem would arise.

The RCMP detachment in Tumbler Ridge was small, and our office had a great working relationship with the RCMP members there. It was a fairly quiet town, so they always enjoyed our visits and helped out with our files or complaints. On this particular day, I was heading up the Murray River to Kinuseo Falls to check for anglers but stopped in at the detachment to say hello. While we were drinking coffee and swapping stories, the members received a call from their dispatch that there was a bear problem in town, and it was apparently right behind their office across from the fire hall. Talk about timing!

One of the Mounties and I hopped into my truck and headed over to the wooded area not far from the detachment. Arriving where the bears had been described to us by the dispatcher, we found a small group of people gathered, peering up into the lodgepole pine trees at not one, but three black bears. A sow with two young cubs.

The bears were not causing any real problems at the time, other than wandering through town. They had climbed trees when they became the focus of attention by townspeople and barking dogs. As such, these bears were likely good candidates for relocation. Fortunately, I had my tranquillizing equipment with me, due to having the culvert trap set across town at another black bear complaint and had planned on checking that trap before leaving the area for the day.

The crowd was growing, so for everyone's safety, I wanted to deal with these bears as quickly as possible. Extra caution was required in a situation like this because the sow would be protecting her cubs. With interested bystanders looking on and wanting to help out, it would become difficult to watch the safety of all the people and animals involved.

I left my constable friend on-site to monitor the bears and onlookers and quickly drove across town to fetch my culvert live trap that luckily had not captured my other target bear yet. I needed the trap to hold the bears in, once they were drugged and ready for transport.

The bears peered curiously down at us from above while we quickly came up with a capture plan. We would dart the sow first, and the cubs would stay treed with their momma safely held in the trap. Cubs of the year, once treed, will rarely climb down unless all people have vacated the area, and they feel safe enough to do so. They will, however, climb higher into a tree if pushed by any disturbances.

I advised the onlookers what was about to transpire and to stay back a safe distance, as a bear startled by a painful dart can come out of a tree very fast and be on the ground before the drug starts to take effect. The sow was up a different tree than the cubs, so I hoped darting her would not startle the cubs into climbing higher. The cubs were small, and safely darting them without causing injury would be difficult, even at close range.

The aluminum darts used for tranquillizing bears hit quite hard and inject the drug pretty aggressively. When the dart hits the animal, the inertia causes a small charge to detonate within the aluminum tube, and a plunger in the tube is blown forward, injecting the drug quickly. A small steel barb hooks beneath the hide, preventing the dart from popping back out when the drug is forcefully injected into muscle. All this action occurs within a second once the trigger is pulled on the tranquillizer gun; therefore, the injection hit is usually quite startling to a bear quietly lying in a tree.

I recalled one occasion when I had darted a bear sitting in a tree fifteen feet from the ground. When the dart hit it in the rump, it launched itself from the tree, landed on all fours and took off running. I never found where the bear had run to, or where it had gone down from the drug. Therefore, I was always cautious when drugging bears that were not secure.

Anyway, the sow was roughly twenty-five feet from the ground, and I quietly took a position below her that provided a good view of her nearest hindquarter. I took aim and let the dart fly. At the impact, the sow let out a startled grunt and climbed a few feet higher. Within five minutes she was showing signs of the drug, and soon she fell down through the branches to the ground, immobilized. Bears are surprisingly resilient animals and can take physical punishment better than most animal species. They can take falls that would cause serious injury to you or me, then get up and run away unscathed. It is not uncommon for a bear hit by a vehicle to get up and run off unharmed. With the empty trap sitting nearby, I removed the dart and we lifted her in. I affixed a plastic identification tag to her ear, placed a protective cloth over her open eyes, then quietly closed the trap door. One down, two to go.

The cubs were perched about the same distance from the ground as their mother had been, and I was concerned what the second cub might do if startled when the first cub was darted. I took aim at the nearest cub's hind end, which offered a very small target. Using a smaller dart with less drug, the tranquillizer gun let out a *pffft* as I touched the trigger, and the dart placed itself perfectly into the little bear's rump. The cub let out a bawl and quickly climbed higher, taking its sibling with it. As the darted cub became limp and fell from the branches, the second cub became startled and climbed even higher up the skinny lodgepole pine. We attended to the drugged cub, and watched its sibling climb even higher, realizing we had a height problem on our hands. It was now hiding among the branches an honest sixty feet up the tree, and there was no way I could accurately or safely dart the little cub at that distance.

Once the first cub had been placed inside the live trap with its mother, we pondered the height problem, wondering how we could get the little guy out of the tree safely. While standing there we looked across the street toward the fire hall, and a crazy thought came to mind. Fire halls have big trucks with tall ladders. ... What if? Well, nothing ventured, nothing gained, so my constable counterpart quick-stepped over to the station and disappeared inside. A short time later he came out with a big grin on his face, and one of the tall louvred bay doors began to open.

One of the engines slowly rolled out of the bay and a siren let out a short "whoop-whoop" as it crossed the road toward us. The driver wore a humongous grin, and the onlooking crowd hooted with excitement as the truck approached. Lying atop the engine was one of those hydraulic extending/articulating ladders that I'm sure reaches a mile into the sky. Oh boy, this was going to get interesting now, very interesting.

The driver parked the big fire engine and jumped down to the ground with us, enthusiastically asking what the plan of attack was. I pointed out the small black speck of a bear cub high in the nearby pine tree. I asked if his ladder could reach that height and if he could get me close enough to dart it among the trees. He responded with a resounding, "No problem!"

At that point, I knew there was a problem, though. ... I was going to be the lucky person who had to climb up that monster ladder to deal with the cub at an ungodly height. But the stage was set, the crowd was watching, and there was nowhere to go now ... except up. I had made my bed, and now I had to lay in it!

While the engine was positioned accordingly, and the outriggers placed for stability, I began preparing the darting equipment again. But as I squatted down to prepare the dart load, my right knee popped and sent me to the ground in serious pain. I had had a minor issue with my knee when I was a kid, but nothing like this. Something was wrong with it, and I had a crowd of onlookers waiting for me to rescue the cub ... not to mention the massive fire ladder now extending out into the treetops on my behalf. I gathered my legs under me and tried to stand, but my knee would not support my weight. I could barely stand, let alone walk or climb ladders or deal with bears. I was not sure if I could pull this off with my knee in this condition, but I had no choice.

I relayed my knee problem to the constable but said I would carry on, not wanting to draw attention to the ever-widening yellow streak running down the length of my back. Carrying the tranquillizer gun, I painfully hobbled over to the fire engine and began the climb, realistically needing an escalator at that point, not a tranquillizing gun. I held onto the ladder railing with a death grip as I began my ascent, wondering how I had gotten myself into this ridiculous, painful predicament.

Keith and bear trap just after releasing black bears

The higher I got, the more the ladder bounced, and I realized that using the tranquillizer gun safely at this height was a no-go; I was not going to be able to safely let go of the railing in order to accurately discharge the gun. But as I neared the cub, I figured I might be able to direct the ladder close enough to the cub to grab it by relaying directions to the engine operator below. With my new plan taking shape, I turned and hobbled back down the ladder, left my tranquillizing gun at the bottom, and asked the firefighter to get me as close as he could to the bear.

Up I went again, and when I reached the tip of the ladder, it began to extend upward toward the cub. At this height, when the angle of the ladder needed to be changed it would ferociously bounce around, scaring the bejesus out of me while I held on for dear life. Doing my best to focus on the bear cub and not the height, I pushed away thoughts of slipping off the ladder and the sudden stop waiting at the bottom, which might end my days. I held on with white knuckles while the ladder was manoeuvred into place immediately below the cub. I had but one chance, so when I was within five feet of the little black furball, I reached up with my free arm and grabbed the cub by the scruff of the neck, pulling it off the tree it was desperately clinging to. With the last remnants of my intestinal fortitude, I hung onto the ladder with one hand and a bawling bear cub with the other, while the ladder was retracted and lowered to the truck level.

Somehow, I managed to get off the ladder to the ground while barely able to walk, and as I hobbled back to the trap with cub in hand, the crowd broke into a resounding volley of cheers. As the yellow stripe down my back began to dissipate, I placed the fully awake cub into the trap with its sleeping mother and sibling. Then I began to realize I had a very real problem with my knee.

With the crowd peering into the trap at the family of bears, I thanked the fire department and RCMP member who had helped me and gathered up my gear. I said my goodbyes to the crowd, then headed down the road for my final job of the day, releasing the bears. An hour later I held the trap door open as a woozy sow black bear led her two little cubs out of the trap and trotted off into the bush. Satisfied with the outcome, I arrived home for a late supper with my knee swelled up like a balloon. At the table, I relayed the story to Shannon and the kids and tried to downplay my knee. However, my hobbling gait betrayed me, and Shannon knew better.

Fast forward one year. I lay asleep on an operating table in Grande Prairie having a badly torn meniscus cartilage removed from my right knee. Oh, the joys of CO bear work!!

33

UNSOLVED

More often than not, wildlife cases can be difficult to solve. The common witnesses are trees and birds, and they can't speak. The victims are wildlife, and they can't speak either. Like all enforcement agencies though, COs rely heavily on the public to help solve cases when possible. But unlike criminal cases, which often involve human victims and witnesses, COs are often left to solve a case with only the physical evidence found in the bush and nothing more. We would always hope that "loose lips would sink ships," and that a story might surface to point us in the right direction. This would not often happen though, so cases would go unsolved. Those cases really bothered me over the years, and unfortunately, there were more than just a few.

The cases that bothered me most were those that involved shot and left animals. During my Peace Country tenure, I investigated dozens of bull moose and mule deer bucks that were shot and left due to illegal antler size. The shooter would kill the animal from a distance thinking or hoping the antlers possessed the minimum required number of points to be legal. Once realizing the animal was not legal, they would simply walk away to find another animal. If nobody witnessed the event or saw a vehicle in the area, the case would often go unsolved. Even if a shell casing was retrieved at the scene, there was often no firearm to compare it to forensically. The animal wastage was very real and saddening.

During the summer of 1984, I received a call from a young man who had been hiking on Sugarloaf Mountain, just east of Merritt. He asked me if the hunting season was open for deer at the time, as he had come across a deer that had been shot and left. I advised him no, the season did not open until September. He stated that the deer had been dressed out, and a few articles had been left with the deer; thus, it appeared the culprits planned to return. I asked the fellow if he would be willing to take me to the site, and he agreed.

I dropped my mundane office paperwork and quickly headed out the office door. It was a fairly warm late July day, so I knew that if, in fact, the culprits were planning to return and claim the deer carcass, they would not be gone long. Normally, game animals do not get dressed out by the shooter if they have no intention of returning.

The young hiker climbed into my Toyota 4X4 work truck and began to explain the details. He directed me toward Nicola Lake, then south along the base of Sugarloaf Mountain toward the present Coquihalla Highway hill that heads to the Okanagan. He had been hiking cross country through the dry grass and sagebrush-covered ridges, and the only way he knew how to get back to the deer was by using the same off-road route he had earlier hiked.

The little Toyota 4x4 was the right vehicle for the job and easily climbed the slopes once we left the gravel back road. I did not like going off-road, as vehicle tires can easily cause damage to delicate grassy hillsides, but we really had no choice if he was going to lead me to the deer. I locked in the hubs, put it in low range (or bull-low, as I liked to call it), and slowly climbed up the grassy hillsides and draws. Leaving very little sign of our passing, we reached the timbered upper slopes. Gradually the slope lessened and we began to weave our way through the fir and poplar forest. I was actually pretty amazed at how he navigated us through the forested area, then finally told me that we had arrived. Back in those days, there was no GPS available to guide folks back to a remote area, where the forest looks pretty much the same in all directions. He did well to get us there without a hitch.

He led me to a doe mule deer a short distance from the 4x4. It had been shot and gutted. The paunch was lying a short distance away, but the hide had not been removed. Lying on the deer was a tee-shirt used as a rag, as well as a folding knife. Somebody was definitely coming back for this deer. It was a warm day, and the shooter would know the meat would sour if left in the midday heat for very long.

I outlined my plan to the hiker and advised that I wanted to sit and wait for the culprits to return. I wasted no time taking a few evidence photos and pulled the truck to where it could not be seen, positioning it in an area where we could see the kill site through the brush. I knew of a logging road not too far away, which the culprit had likely used to access the area, and odds were that they would likely come back in that way. There could have been a number of reasons the deer was left. Perhaps the person was alone and wanted to go for help (that was the likely reason), or perhaps they had hunted on foot a long distance from their vehicle and had left to retrieve it. Regardless, I doubted they would take very long to return. I walked through the bush toward the road and found that we were not far from it at all. Looking around, I made a mental note of where we were in relation to it.

Quickstepping back to the truck, we settled into the cab and quietly waited. I outlined to the young man how, for safety reasons, I wanted him to wait in the truck if the culprits showed up, and then we discussed his discovery in more detail. We agreed that finding the deer was definitely a one-off, as the odds of him coming across the downed deer in the forest were low.

Mule deer doe discovered by hiker on Sugarloaf Mountain

We had waited for about fifteen minutes when the hiker advised that he had to be back in town for an important appointment that he could not miss. I advised him that he had failed to mention that little detail earlier. He apologized, saying that he thought we would be headed back to town by now. He was adamant, so I felt I should accommodate him given the information he had provided to me thus far. However, I knew I should not chance going out to the road that the shooter might be coming back in on. Therefore, I chose to drive him back down through the grassy slopes the way we had come in, then return via the backroad where I might encounter the culprit. It would have to be very quick, but I thought I might be able to do it within thirty minutes or so.

Knowing the risk of leaving the deer and possibly missing the culprit, I quickly hopped out of the truck, signed and dated one of my business cards, cut a small slit with my knife in one of the deer's hindquarters, folded the card up, and slid it into the hindquarter near the pelvis. That way, when or if I encountered the shooter, I could identify the deer. It was a hastily designed plan, but I was low on options. Without hanging around very long to think about it, I trotted back to the truck, took it out of low range and headed for town.

I did not feel good about pulling away from the deer, but we quickly made our way back to town, where I got the man's contact details and dropped him off. I abruptly put the pedal to the metal and headed up the Aspen Grove Highway to where the logging road made its exit.

Given the short time it had taken to return, I felt confident that I might encounter the culprits coming out with the deer on the logging road, so I mentally prepared myself for the check. I travelled alone the vast majority of time in Merritt and had to complete road checks alone on a regular basis. However, I never knew what I might encounter, what a bad guy's personality might be, or what that person may have experienced that day. I had checked people alone previously who had experienced a serious domestic dispute and were more than just a little agitated at the world. I was just the guy in uniform for them to take their frustrations out on. Therefore, I was always a little anxious about what I might encounter.

As I reached the location along the road that I recognized as the spot where I had walked out from the deer, I realized that it was not very far from the highway at all. Travelling between the deer kill and the freedom of the highway would not take long for the culprits. Sure enough, I could see vehicle tracks that had left the road through the ditch, and I suddenly had a sick feeling in my stomach.

Walking into the woods to where the deer had lain, I was not surprised when I found it gone, along with the rag and knife. The person(s) must have returned at the very time we were driving back down the hill toward town; otherwise, I likely would have encountered them coming back out on the road. I was more than a little upset with myself for letting a sure thing slip through my fingers, but helping the complainant who took the time to report it was important to me.

I quickly checked the area for any other evidence, but found nothing except vague tire marks left in the dry forest duff and roadway. The culprits had turned their vehicle toward the highway, so I knew they were long gone. They had made it to the freedom of the pavement where they could have gone who-knows-where. I had no idea which direction they had gone, and by the time I reached the highway, it had been long enough that they could have gotten to town, headed south, or taken any sideroad off the highway. I was stumped.

The deer had not been wasted like the countless "shot and left" files I later investigated in the Peace Country, as the deer appeared to have been taken for use by the person who had killed it. However, it was still out-of-season and illegal. It rattled me that I had been so close to catching the responsible party but had missed my opportunity. The culprits probably got a real surprise the day they butchered that deer or cooked a roast and found my business card tucked inside the meat. Unfortunately, that's as close as I ever got to catching the responsible party or solving the case.

34

BLACK AS
COAL

During the late winter months in the Peace Country, a strange moose event would often unfold. The long-legged critters would start homesteading right on people's doorsteps for a couple of different reasons ... food and predators.

Much to its chagrin, over the years the BC farming community has provided a steady source of food for ungulates—deer, elk and moose—that roam their fields and woodlands. In many cases, alfalfa fields and hay stackyards have provided ungulates with feed to make it through harsh winters that they might not have otherwise survived. However, even in "normal" winters, ungulates regularly invaded haystacks and caused problems. Once attracted to a winter food source, such as baled hay, moose specifically, can become quite possessive and aggressive if pushed.

Moose also often moved in close to homes in late winter for health reasons, and it was not completely uncommon to find one lying right at a home's doorstep. Once moose become malnourished, or an infestation of ticks makes them unhealthy, they will move in close to human activity (homes) for safety.

There, predators such as wolves and coyotes, who shy away from human presence, are less likely to harass or cause them harm.

Many winter moose stories come to mind, some of which I chuckle about every time I recall them, but one event, on a frigid Peace Country winter night near Groundbirch back in 1996, really stands out:

A big old bull moose that had not yet shed its four foot spread of antlers (ungulates shed their antlers every winter and grow new ones the following summer), had been putting the run on a rancher every time he went out to his stackyard to feed hay to his cows. If he stepped off his tractor, the bull would lower his head and charge him. He had tried everything to scare the bull away, but it had no intention of leaving the best food source it had found that winter. Speaking of good food, deer, elk and moose will tell ranchers, real quick, who has the best-baled hay during winter months.

Moose are the least intrusive of all ungulates around stackyards, and although they are the biggest, they actually cause the least amount of damage to the fences and bales. They are good jumpers and don't drag their rear legs on the wire when clearing a fence, unlike elk that are lazy jumpers. Elk tend to drag their back legs and will pull down wire fences as they lazily hop over them. No ... moose are good jumpers with their long gangly legs.

Moose also have good table manners around baled hay. Deer and elk paw at hay bales to separate out the leafy chaff from the stems and waste a lot of hay in the process (yes, I know ungulates do not have paws, they have hooves). They will also lie, urinate and defecate on the hay, making it unpalatable for livestock. Moose, on the other hand, having a more refined sense of table etiquette, will stand in one place and simply eat a big hole into the end of a round bale, wasting very little.

So back to the big bull moose. The rancher had tried everything short of shooting it with no success, so he called me for help. He advised that the bull was sometimes there during the daytime but was most often around in the darker hours. As such, I attended a couple of times during the day but never set eyes on the bull, so I decided a night excursion was the way to ultimately deal with this big guy. There was no way I was going to try to drug a moose in the dark, so, unfortunately, I had no choice but to pack my rifle.

Darkness comes early during the winter months in the Peace Country, so as soon as supper was over, I hopped in the truck and headed to Groundbirch. I had a quick coffee with the rancher and laid out my foolproof plan about sneaking into the stackyard. I figured I'd be able to pick out the moose's silhouette in the wintery darkness, hit my flashlight, then send the big antlered willow sniffer to the big stackyard in the sky. It seemed pretty simple in my mind. Although I really preferred not to destroy the bull, I was left with no other option. He was very aggressive, and the meat from him would not go to waste; I would distribute it among local needy families.

Gulping down the last of the hot black coffee, I headed out to the truck to get my rifle and flashlight, then walked over to the stackyard. It was completely dark outside now, black as coal, and I began to wonder how wise the plan I had hatched really was. After all, I was going in after a half-ton, sharp antlered, aggressive bull moose that was also black. I figured this was probably a losing poker hand at best, but I had come this far, no point in turning back.

The stackyard was large with multiple rows of round bales stacked two high. (The bottom bale sits on end and the top bale lies on its side. This stacking arrangement sheds rain and protects both bales from the weather.) The eight-foot-high rows were spaced with narrow alleyways, just wide enough for a tractor to manoeuvre. It was also the perfect set-up to provide cover and a sense of safety for the moose, not to mention an all-you-can-eat nightly buffet.

I knew I had to get close to the bull to get the deed done in the dark, so I went into stealth mode and began slowly creeping my way down an alleyway. On high alert for any movement, I crept my way along, expecting to see the dark bulky outline of the bull standing in front of me at any moment. I had worked my way down one alleyway, then turned and began working my way down another. I was seriously questioning my sanity creeping along in the pitch-black darkness, when without warning the area around me came alive with thundering black bodies.

There must have been a dozen moose thundering off in all directions. I had crept right into the middle of an entire herd of moose and all hell broke loose. I never saw an antler or any other identifiable body part, just big black hulks charging past me. I didn't even attempt to turn my flashlight on, as it would likely have added to the chaos. With animals all around me running full tilt, I wasn't about to chance a night-time shot, so I just wedged my backside into the nearest bale and let the rodeo play itself out.

After thirty seconds or so I finally shone the flashlight around, holding onto a glimmer of hope that perhaps the big bull moose would be aggressive enough to hold back and challenge the two-legged intruder. But no, the stackyard was completely and totally vacant except for a six-foot pathetic dough-head standing there holding a flashlight. Totally deflated, I shuffled my way back toward my truck, stopping once to quickly check behind me with my flashlight, but the hay yard was still and empty.

I broke the news to the rancher and thanked my lucky stars for still being in one piece. Neither the rancher nor I ever did see the bull moose again (I actually never did lay eyes on it). That herd of moose and I all got a heavy dose of fear put into us that dark winter's night. I mean, why would any sane moose want to return to a stackyard where a two-legged lunatic was on the loose in the dark!

EPILOGUE

On that still, Peace Country winter night in 1996, the four-and-a-half-foot wingspan effortlessly carried the one-kilogram feathered hunter silently through the starlight over the snow-covered stubble field through the pitch black. This was his time, the night. His round night eyes and dished face peered beyond the black flatness of the field toward his goal. Stretching forward with his thick feathered legs, the eight black talons reached outward like two-inch scimitars as he flared his wings and tail feathers. The cold winter air rippled through his primary feathers as the Great Grey slowed and settled on top of the forty-foot telephone pole without a sound. His stomach was only half full, and it was time for another meal.

At nine and a half years old, Strix nebulosi had hunted from this same perch over two hundred times previously. One of his favorites. He folded his sculpted wings in tightly against his sides and ruffled his grey breast feathers against the minus thirty-degree night, then settled in to watch for movement. The little white bow tie positioned slightly below his beak bore stark contrast to his slate grey body, giving an air of prestige to the night hunter. It was calm and clear, a perfect night to hunt one of his favorite prey animals, Microtus pennsylvanicus, a meadow vole. Positioning himself so that his piercing yellow eyes glared menacingly down the two-high rows of round bales set out in front of him, the big owl began his nightly routine of waiting patiently for movement among the bales.

His head pivoted to the right thirty degrees as he focused on the ground near a cow moose shuffling among the bales below. The quiet footfalls of the nine-hundred-pound black body in the alfalfa made it difficult to hear the vole moving along the one-inch chaff tunnel from its den nearby. He knew it would not be long before one of the many moose feeding below pushed a vole from the safety of the hay. Straining to bring in the sounds of ground movement, a yellow light suddenly streamed down the steps from a nearby farmhouse door pulling his gaze from the stackyard. A murmuring voice followed the light down the steps.

Invisible in the darkness, the predator swiveled his head and watched the human figure move away from the house to the CO truck parked nearby. A dim light shone from the cab of the truck, as the owl's ears picked up the metallic "snick" of a rifle bolt being closed. The cab light extinguished itself and the human form moved quietly past the base of the high perch to the gate below, where the faintest creak of an old hinge hit the Great Grey like fingernails on a chalkboard.

Following the human form that moved in a slow, predatory-like fashion down a laneway between the bales, the big owl rotated its head back toward the stackyard taking in the night scene with silent study. The human stopped at the end of the row of bales briefly and peered blindly back toward the perch, then slowly began to move back through the adjoining laneway while the Great Grey's large eyes followed the human's quiet movements. Forty feet now separated the human from the ten moose that fed quietly below the owl, all with their long noses pressed into two-foot holes they had eaten into the ends of round bales. The moose had good table manners, wasting little.

The big bull pulled his long black snout from the bale and swiveled his four-foot expanse of antlers toward the approaching human form in the alleyway. Boring a hole through the darkness with his dark brown eyes, the bull sensed a presence. The five cows and four calves also swiveled their heads toward the human form, their twelve-inch ears pivoting forward to pick up any sound. Catching a waft of man-scent, the bull spun to his left and lunged forward through a gap between two bales, and the remainder of the herd scattered like flies in the darkness.

The sound of heavy, thundering hooves filled the cold air as the panicked herd bolted through gaps in the bales, over the low cattle fence and out into the winter night. The human stopped and seemed to shrink among the bales, as moose footfalls faded into the dark expanse of empty field. Silence then again descended on the stackyard, as the Great Grey turned his head back toward the human form. A brilliant white beam suddenly pierced the night and seemed to wander aimlessly throughout the stackyard, causing the owl's eyes to close when the beam neared his perch, then went out just as quickly. The human re-appeared once again from among the bales muttering in a low tone, then slowly made his way along the remainder of the laneway toward the gate, now more casually.

Passing near a four-inch vole that struggled to regain its footing on top of the loose hay, the human moved by in the darkness unaware of the rodent's predicament. The vole's pelvis, crushed by a heavy black hoof, caused its short front legs to jack-hammer violently at the ground in a failed attempt to run beneath a bale. Without warning black talons tore through its thin hide, as the vole was lifted from the chaff six feet behind the human. The powerful wings pumped hard four times, then the owl silently reached out for the high perch again.

Stopping and turning abruptly, the human stared blindly back into the dark stackyard searching for the source of the slight sound. Again, the bright white light streamed down the alleyway and meandered through the bales for a short time, then went out. With no perceived movement and only dark stillness remaining, the human finally turned and moved on. While the vole's body relaxed in the death grip, the owl's gaze followed the human through the gate toward the farmhouse. As the CO truck pulled out of the yard and disappeared down the highway into the darkness, the Great Grey uncaringly turned his head back toward the meal at his feet. The vole's partner hidden in the little chaff den was unaware, but the owl's white bow tie seemed to imply that he, like the moose, also had good table manners. He started to feed.

This last tale *could* very well be true. It *was* very dark that cold winter night in the stackyard, and voles love stackyards as much as moose do, and I *did* hear things.

The old adage "The sun comes up and the sun goes down, the hands on the clock go 'round and 'round" infers life can be boring. As a conservation officer though, life was anything but boring. There was always something truly interesting happening, and I enjoyed every minute of it. My time doing CO work deepened my lifelong appreciation of the environment and the flora and fauna that make it home. Relative to the Milky Way's timeclock, none of us spend very long on good old Planet Earth. So I hope what I accomplished as a CO over my short time had a positive effect on our environment in some small fashion, and I hope you enjoyed hearing about a few of those experiences.